MYTHOS TAROT

Guidance from the Greek gods

HELENA ELIAS

ROCKPOOL

A Rockpool book
PO Box 252
Summer Hill
NSW 2130
Australia

rockpoolpublishing.com
Follow us! **f** 🄾 rockpoolpublishing
Tag your images with #rockpoolpublishing

ISBN: 9781922785350

Published in 2023 by Rockpool Publishing
Copyright text and illustrations © Helena Elias 2023
Copyright design © Rockpool Publishing 2023

Design and typsetting by Sara Lindberg, Rockpool Publishing
Edited by Lisa Macken

Printed and bound in China
10 9 8 7 6 5 4 3 2 1

CONTENTS

INTRODUCTION

Mystical direction. Magnificent deities. Mindful decisions. *Mythos Tarot*.

The Greek pantheon consists of divine and semi-divine figures who harken back to the foundation of Western civilisation. First recorded in ancient Greece, these eternal archetypes echo through the ages, singing insights into the heart of what it means to be human.

The truths imbued in this tarot deck are tried and tested. The force of each Greek deity has been carefully tailored to the energy of each card, which keeps open the timeless wisdom of the tarot yet offers novel channels of internal connection influenced by each god or goddess.

Very few of us are as we seem, and it is doubly so for gods. The complexity of their characters means that you may have found strong pairings for a particular god with different cards to this deck's representation. This is to be expected, because even though here they are represented only once each, in their many faces the gods can preside over multiple cards.

The gods are made of both dark and light, embedded in the deep swirls of their characters. I have tried to capture a snapshot of an endless drama in this deck. While I have framed each snapshot to capture some central essence of each deity, I encourage you to find your own connection with the gods as it will allow the tarot to resonate on a greater level with you and will enhance any readings given or received.

If you do dive into historical texts to explore some of these venerable stories you may discover the contradictions inherent in Grecian texts. Many of them are a product of the time, a side-effect of the audience or reinterpretation of a codified oral tradition. If there seems to be a contradiction in this deck it is because I have chosen the path of written history that had the strongest pull to me.

Within the sources I have drawn from it is worth noting that they are often coloured by ancient and modern cultural norms, from patriarchal societies with at times questionable ethics. Through a modern lens some deeds of these deities may appear to be questionable and dark, so you may find a personal interpretation of the god's essence better serves you.

This deck is here to help guide you, orient you towards peace, clarify truths and much more. From experiencing both the written and painted medium in its creation I have felt a deep connection with each card and ancient god in turn. I hope this comes through in the deck and brings you insight, visual connections and joy through the years.

Enjoy the journey.

HELENA ELIAS

HOW TO USE THE CARDS

This deck is based around the traditional tarot. It is made up of 78 cards comprising 22 major arcana and 56 minor arcana cards.

❖ MAJOR ARCANA ❖

The major arcana cards, which frequently champion an Olympian god, are often complex and significant, with the god's pronounced presence in your life influencing the reading. They often represent overarching life themes and answers for the long term.

❖ MINOR ARCANA ❖

The minor arcana cards relate to shorter or more specific aspects of your life and are reflective of your current situation. They are split into four suits with focus points, and the number of cards in each suit in your reading can affect the overarching theme and story the gods are trying to tell you. The four suits are:

- Wands, representing fire, passion and energy.
- Coins, representing earth, materialistic elements and finance.
- Cups, representing water, emotions and intuition.
- Swords, representing air, intellect and thoughts.

While this book is a guide to the meanings behind the traditional tarot and the gods guiding the card, this is just the beginning. Real power comes from tapping in to your intuition and wisdom, to your personal connection and interpretation. As you become familiar with this deck, find the way that suits you the most in reading it.

The *Mythos Tarot* has been designed with options for risen and fallen positions, traditionally called 'upright' and 'reversed'. You may find this way of reading calls to you, especially as you gain a more intimate connection to the gods over time. Keep an eye out for combinations of particular gods and their relations to each other; you may find your inner understanding is speaking to a deep connection between them, which will provide additional insight to your reading. Before beginning your reading, set an intention and focus on what you'd like answered, calling out to the pantheon as you do so. Keep your request precise and specific.

You will find different spreads call to you for different readings and new ones will come with time, but below are three examples of how the deck can be read.

◆ TRINITY SPREAD ◆

The trinity spread is a linear path, sequence or cause and effect. The gods may each be overlooking a different aspect of your life or they may be working in unison together, so trust your intuition about how they interact with each other.

- Option 1, card 1: past, card 2: present, card 3: future.
- Option 2, card 1: situation, card 2: action, card 3: outcome.
- Option 3, card 1: you, card 2: your path, card 3: your potential.

◆ DIRECT SPREAD ◆

The direct spread can be an excellent way to become familiar with this deck and establish a deep and personal connection with the gods within. Approach your question with focused intention, and see who from the pantheon is watching over you and trying to send you a message.

◆ OLYMPIAN SPREAD ◆

In this 12-card spread each card relates to an Olympian. If you pull an Olympian within this set it holds extra weight in the meaning. A second way to use this spread is to future scry for the next 12 months from the time of reading, with each card drawn resonating with a month.

- Card 1, Zeus: how do you define yourself?
- Card 2, Hera: what issues from the past are affecting current relationships?
- Card 3, Poseidon: what are the challenges you must overcome?
- Card 4, Demeter: what requires more balance?
- Card 5, Apollo: how can you let go of your fears?
- Card 6, Artemis: how can you open up to others?
- Card 7, Hermes: what next step must you take on your journey?
- Card 8, Athena: what must you do to be fair to yourself and those around you?
- Card 9, Hephaestus: how are you releasing your creative self?
- Card 10, Aphrodite: what is your heart's desire?
- Card 11, Ares: how do you confront conflict?
- Card 12, Dionysus: how can you let more joy enter your life?

MAJOR
ARCANA

0. THE FOOL

PAN

GOD OF THE WILD, SHEPHERDS AND MISCHIEF

Pan was a mischievous god whose laughter was consistently changing. Eternally roaming to the sound of his choice musical notes, he chased nymphs and created novelty.

RISEN

BEGINNINGS, INNOCENCE, FREE SPIRIT, SPONTANEITY, TRAVEL, FOOLISHNESS

You have reached the beginning of a journey and Pan's wild spirit burns within you. There is opportunity and potential ahead of the journey, and you are about to take your first step into the unknown. In this new adventure there is a calling to channel Pan's free-spirited nature and leave behind any fear, regret or anxiety. There is a leap of faith to be taken, but you are ready for it so step off the base of earth and fly with the wild music. Release your inner child and the changing joys of Pan and step into the unknown with a lively greeting for all of the opportunities that await you.

This card in your reading could represent new relationships or the opportunity to explore fresh experiences. Changes in your career or life path may appear like openings in a forest, and this is the perfect time to dance to Pan's music along a new path. If others think you are wild for dancing, treat them with love and compassion for they are simply not able to hear the music.

FALLEN

HOLDING BACK, RECKLESSNESS, GULLIBILITY, DISTRACTION, APATHY

Pan's pipes are playing wildly in your ears and may be carrying you away with the ferocious fever of his music. Take a step back to consider whether you're taking too many risks or acting recklessly. There is a joy in spontaneity and adventures, but be careful of a disregard of dignity and well-being: your own and that of others. There are ways to keep the free spirit of Pan in your life, and now is the time to take a moment to consider how to do that.

For your career and finances this is a time to reflect before you act lest the music of Pan's pipes leads you astray. On the other hand, you may be blocking out Pan's pipes completely and not hearing the joy and carefree music of life, coming instead to a stale standstill. Remember to keep joy in your life and find ways to ensure that play has a place there.

I. THE MAGICIAN

HECATE

(HEKATE) GODDESS OF MAGIC, WITCHCRAFT, THE MOON, GHOSTS AND NECROMANCY

Hecate was a powerful second-generation Titan goddess who was feared by even such as Zeus for her strong powers within magic. She spent most of her time in the underworld as companion to Persephone, assisting to keep away evil spirits. She was either single or triple formed, standing back to back to look in all directions at once from a crossroad.

RISEN

WILLPOWER, DESIRE, CREATION, MANIFESTATION, INFLUENCE, INTELLECT

The triple-faced goddess Hecate, bringer of magic, witchcraft and the moon, entreats a powerful force to enter your life to help you manifest your desires, dreams or destiny. This is a card of pure willpower, weaving all elements together with the demands of desire. It is time to harness your full potential and aim to find the best version of yourself.

You must be clear about your needs and wants, the what and the why. When you have set your sights on your dream, be committed and avoid distractions to make real your imaginings. You are currently a manifestation powerhouse and can harness Hecate's power to mould your future into what you most desire. Now is not the time to hold back.

FALLEN

TRICKERY, ILLUSIONS, OUT OF TOUCH, MANIPULATION, UNUSED ABILITY

There is currently a block on your power, and Hecate has appeared in your reading to assist you to find a way forward. You may be trying to move forward with your dreams but are not taking action and are unclear on why that is so. It is time to revisit your goals and make sure that both the end goal and the journey you are looking to take are aligned. This could be a warning from Hecate that the end goal may not be aligned with your calling and to revise what you wish for.

This card can also signify trickery and manipulation. It could be a time to reflect and make sure you are not deceiving others, or perhaps yourself. Always check back in to make sure you're working for the good of others and not just for your sole benefit. Perhaps someone who seems to have your best interests at heart is in fact working against your needs, if not your wants. Take time to affirm what those needs are along with other people's intentions towards you.

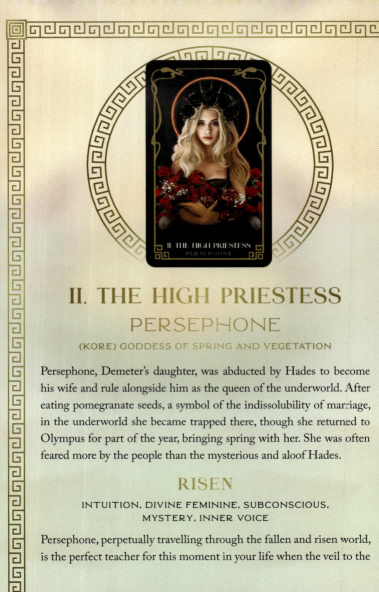

II. THE HIGH PRIESTESS

PERSEPHONE

(KORE) GODDESS OF SPRING AND VEGETATION

Persephone, Demeter's daughter, was abducted by Hades to become his wife and rule alongside him as the queen of the underworld. After eating pomegranate seeds, a symbol of the indissolubility of marriage, in the underworld she became trapped there, though she returned to Olympus for part of the year, bringing spring with her. She was often feared more by the people than the mysterious and aloof Hades.

RISEN

INTUITION, DIVINE FEMININE, SUBCONSCIOUS, MYSTERY, INNER VOICE

Persephone, perpetually travelling through the fallen and risen world, is the perfect teacher for this moment in your life when the veil to the underworld and your subconscious is thin. You have an opportunity to access your subconscious mind and the inner wisdom found deep within your soul. Allow Persephone to be your guide and connect you with your intuition through your chosen form of spiritual journeying. Find answers from within rather than without.

The divine feminine energy of Persephone is strong at the moment, so it is important to balance the masculine and feminine energies in your life. It may be important to embrace the feminine, leaning in to creation, nurturing and empathy.

FALLEN

HIDDEN MOTIVES, SUPERFICIALITY, CONFUSION, WITHDRAWAL, DISSONANCE, REPRESSED FEELINGS

Your intuition has been speaking to you but you have been ignoring the call. Persephone has turned up in your reading to help guide you back to your inner voice, so take time to listen to what it is trying to tell you. A new path is waiting to be illuminated, and there is a calling to be more authentic. Remember your personal values and follow your gut intuition, making sure you are not prioritising other people's approval over your own wisdom. As with the risen position of this card the veil between your subconscious and the underworld is thin, so it is time to take Persephone's guidance and traverse both realms on your spiritual journeying.

Follow your feelings when it comes to romance, as difficulties may arise if you try to force things. You may feel out of touch and kept in the dark, so it is important to step back and take in everything that you can. Authenticity and honesty are key at this time.

III. THE EMPRESS

HERA

GODDESS OF MARRIAGE, WOMEN AND CHILDBIRTH

Hera, one of the 12 Olympians, was the queen of the gods, ruling alongside her husband Zeus. In a marriage full of infidelity, she pursued with a vindictive hatred the women he was involved with. She was a strong and powerful goddess who presided over fertility and marriage.

RISEN

MOTHERHOOD, FERTILITY, NATURE, FEMININITY, NURTURING, ABUNDANCE, CREATIVITY

Hera was a goddess of women and femininity and is here to help you tap into yours, regardless of gender identity. Both masculine and feminine energy are important for balance, and at this time your creative, nurturing and sensual sides need to be called to the forefront and celebrated. You are in a period of growth, and Hera entreats you to be grateful for the bounty around you. It is a reminder to connect with what makes you happy in life and to take care of yourself. Use Hera's strong, confident, feminine energy to mine your own internal power, which will shine through to those around you.

There is a strong urge to care for those around you, as this is a time of love and support. Quality time is important, and this card can indicate a new member being added to your family in whatever form that means to you.

FALLEN

DEPENDENCE, SMOTHERING, EMPTINESS, NOSINESS, CREATIVE BLOCKS, DISHARMONY

While a powerful and loving goddess, Hera also had a very jealous, destructive side. Instead of channeling her feminine, loving power you are drawing her insecurities, potentially becoming overprotective, co-dependent and controlling. It is time to take a step back and breathe, revisiting your relationships with independence, trust and compassion.

Hera in the fallen position may also be indicative of the reverse, with a loss of independence, and a feeling of being smothered. It is time to take on her willpower and strength to build confidence in your decisions and actions. Your self-image may be low, and it is time to remember that you too are a powerful, shining power. Learn to love yourself again and rediscover your inner and outer beauty. Self-love and self-care are priorities.

If you are experiencing a creative block, time out in nature can help to ease this.

IV. THE EMPEROR

ZEUS

GOD OF THE SKY, WEATHER, LAW, DESTINY AND FATE

Zeus, the king of the gods and one of the 12 Olympians, was a powerful god associated strongly with thunder and lightning. He shared rule over the human world with his two brothers Hades and Poseidon after the Titanomachy, a 10-year battle to defeat their father Cronus and the Titans. He married Hera, the queen of the gods, although he also had many relations with other gods and mortals.

RISEN

AUTHORITY, ESTABLISHMENT, STRUCTURE, FATHER FIGURE, CONTROL, PROTECTION, DISCIPLINE

Zeus, the king and father of the gods and a powerful leader, shines strongly in your life right now. With his power you are adopting his role by providing for those around you, protecting and defending your loved ones. You are falling into leadership easily and may feel comfortable directing with a firm hand. Strategy, logic and methodical processes are tools for pursuing goals. This card indicates that hard work will be noticed, with recognition and status as the rewards.

Zeus is a hard task master without time for frivolity, so this may be a moment to ask whether you are being too hard on yourself or on other people around you. You may find at work or in other life activities you have been called to a roll of power, so now is the time to channel Zeus and his wisdom to bring leadership and clarity to the project.

This card also may represent a father figure in your life or someone with high expectations of you.

FALLEN

TYRANNY, RIGIDITY, COLDNESS, DOMINANCE, STUBBORNNESS, CONTROL

Zeus is not always a kind or fair ruler, and when his favour is turned from you the full brunt of his displeasure will be known. There may be abused authoritative power in your life at the moment that could potentially manifest in a possessive partner or overreach of power. Alternatively, this could be originating from you, so it is time to step back and analyse how you have been to those around you and the role power plays in your life. You neither need to take it from others nor need to give your power away.

Drawing The Emperor card could be an indication you need to step up to an abuse of authority or seek your own way to escape the confines of someone else's rigid box. If you harness the strength and power of Zeus your efforts will lead to success. This card can also represent discontent around a fatherly figure and a need to instigate more heartfelt conversations around problems. Like Zeus's and Hera's own turbulent relationship, this card can indicate one partner controlling the other or being possessive or stubborn. Be careful in your own commitment in relationships, and ensure you are not taking negative action just to rebel against what The Emperor card and Zeus represent.

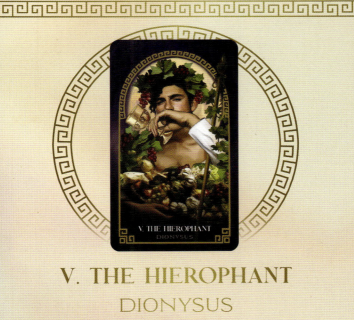

V. THE HIEROPHANT

DIONYSUS

(DIONYSOS) GOD OF WINE, CHAOS, ECSTASY AND THE THEATRE

Dionysus was one of the 12 Olympians, a later edition brought in by his father Zeus. He had the power to inspire and create ecstasy, and as the god of theatre was an important figure in art and literature.

RISEN

REBELLION, SUBVERSIVENESS, NEW APPROACHES, CHAOS, OPEN UNCONVENTIONALITY, NONCONFORMITY

In the chaotic ways of Dionysus, he has flipped the card of The Hierophant and in this risen position is here to tempt you into breaking free of the shackles of convention. He may have appeared in your reading because you are feeling restricted and constrained by structures and rules so has came forth to help you try to break free. It is time to inject extra excitement into your normal life and relationships. You may want to break with traditional structure, social norms and rigid rules, but if those around you do not understand this need for freedom let Dionysus give you the strength to think for yourself and take action for what is right for you unconfined by how others want you to act. Opening your mind and horizons will help you live by your own rules while still following your personal values to remain generous and kind to those around you.

FALLEN

TRADITION, CONFORMITY, MORALITY, ETHICS, BELIEFS, CONVENTIONALITY

Dionysus turned from you indicates you need to put freedom and chaos aside to learn fundamental principles from a trusted source. This is the perfect time to find a mentor or guide to teach you about new beliefs, especially within a structured setting. Perhaps you are in turn the teacher or mentor, honouring your position to share your knowledge. Away from the chaos of Dionysus's court you are staying within convention. There has been turbulence in your life recently, and staying on a well-known path will allow you to grow without having the distractions of new experiences.

This is a period of learning and progression, and if you have been seeking to further your knowledge in something this may be a good time to do so. Don't rock the boat or commit to risky ventures; instead, seek to find comfort in the known.

VI. THE LOVERS

APHRODITE

GODDESS OF BEAUTY, LOVE, DESIRE AND PLEASURE

Aphrodite, most commonly known as the goddess of love and fertility, was one of the 12 Olympians. She was born from sea foam and was worshipped as a goddess of seafaring. She had a great love for Ares but was subjected to an arranged marriage with Hephaestus, and was known to have many mortal lovers.

RISEN

PARTNERSHIPS, DUALITY, UNION, LOVE, DESIRE, SHARED VALUES, CHOICES

The goddess of love, Aphrodite has come into your life to bring open communication and raw honesty as well as a level of vulnerability. Her presence provides a pathway for you to open your heart to your closest loved ones and share your truest feelings in a mutual and powerful way, strengthening your bonds. While this card traditionally signifies a beautiful, shining connection, it can also represent a close friend or family relationship. Ways to empower each other will engender confidence and strength.

Aphrodite also represents choice, as the strongest bonds occur when you remember to choose to love and from the way in which you cultivate it. Another choice you make may be between opposing ideas or finding ways to bring them together to create something that is whole: discovering a balance between advantage and disadvantage, and accepting duality to build unity from which love flows. Now is the time to choose love, both for others and for yourself.

FALLEN

IMBALANCE, ONE-SIDEDNESS, DISHARMONY, VALUE MISALIGNMENT, CONFLICT, DETACHMENT

With Aphrodite in the fallen position you are being warned of potential inner and outer conflicts surrounding you. Reflect on your personal values and your belief system to make sure they are aligned with your highest good. Your romantic or platonic relationships may be out of sync, incurring feelings that can't be shared or mutual. One person may be more emotionally invested, leading to disappointment and insecurity as time goes by. It could also manifest as strained communication and a reluctance to open up emotionally. These are the cornerstones to finding balance once again, so find ways to open up channels of communication and participate in honest discussions about emotions.

The presence of Aphrodite may also be trying to remind you to practise self-love and honour and respect who you are and the value you offer to all around you.

VII. THE CHARIOT
APOLLO

VII. THE CHARIOT
APOLLO

(APOLLON) GOD OF KNOWLEDGE, PROPHECY, ORACLES, SONGS, POETRY, KNOWLEDGE, HEALING, ARCHERY, PLAGUE, DISEASE, PROTECTION OF THE YOUNG

Apollo, one of the great divinities of the ancient Greek age, has a tremendous power to assist you with your current challenges and triumphs. He was one of the 12 gods who ruled Olympus. Replacing Helios as the sun god and twin brother to Artemis, Apollo rode a chariot around the sun to bring light to the world.

RISEN

WILLPOWER, HARD WORK, FOCUS, VICTORY, CONTROL, AMBITION, OVERCOMING OBSTACLES

Like Apollo's own chariot ridden across the sky, The Chariot is a card of movement and direction. Make sure you pay special attention to the road ahead, for your path may not be without challenges. With iron-clad focus and confidence in your abilities you will pass the obstacles ahead. With the movement of Apollo's chariot across the world, this card can also represent your own travel both in the physical and spiritual worlds.

Apollo's strength when channelled can broaden your horizons if you have enough focus and ambition to take control of the reigns and move. He is a god of competition and success, which can bring out a more forceful part of your personality that is a natural part of human nature. This can be used to take charge of your situation – although, importantly, it must be reined in so as to to hinder your path forward.

FALLEN

LACK OF DIRECTION, POWERLESSNESS, BLOCKED BY OBSTACLES, BLUNT FORCE, LACK OF SELF-CONTROL

If this card appears in your reading in reverse you may feel powerless and lacking in direction. You need to pick up the reins of the chariot once more and take control of your own destiny, channelling the powerful force of Apollo to determine your own path.

You may feel the desire to race ahead; have patience. If you have confidence that things will run their natural course then they will run their natural course. Redirect around potential disaster with composure and consideration. Take a step back, and make sure to review your situation before entreating The Chariot to move.

Others people may be taking away your control and leaving you impotent, but it is important to conscientiously take back your power. Without consideration for others you may be led to frustration or uncontrolled aggression, a vice that Apollo often found himself embodying. Set boundaries with the people around you, and with each turning of The Chariot's wheel these will become more entrenched.

VIII. STRENGTH

ATLAS

GOD OF ENDURANCE

Atlas was a Titan god who was sentenced to hold the heavens and sky aloft for eternity after facing defeat in the Titanomachy.

RISEN

STRENGTH, COURAGE, CONFIDENCE, PERSUASION, INFLUENCE, COMPASSION, CONTROL

It takes a lot of strength, endurance and willpower to hold the heavens and sky aloft for eternity, so Atlas's presence in your reading conveys these features in your life at the moment. Stamina and persistence are in abundance, which can come through as a quiet inner power. You have the toughness to conquer any inner doubts or fears you may have. If there are any personal demons you need to conquer now is the time to do it, and if you have any wild ways you may need to balance and tame them. If you have been going through a period of stress, this visit from the god of endurance is a reminder to persevere.

Step up now and support any friends or loved ones who need your help, as you have strength in abundance. Note that in order to take care of others you must first take care of yourself.

FALLEN

VULNERABILITY, SELF-DOUBT, EMOTION, WEAKNESS, INADEQUACY

The path has been long and your endurance strained. Your inner strength is evident if you seek it, so lean upon Atlas as the god of endurance to reach deep and find more of what has always been there. You have an abundance of resilience, which it is time to tap into to get you through these lean times. Focus on the positive and fill your cup with those who build you up, not those who make you feel inadequate. If you need to replenish your energy levels this is a good time to renew and take care of yourself.

Be wary of any explosive emotions you may have been experiencing, channelling any raw emotion so it doesn't harm you or others. Take care of yourself so you can take care of others. Your self-esteem may be low at the moment or manifesting unhappily within your relationships, so take stock and make sure that your anxieties and fears don't prompt you to make an Olympus out of limpets.

IX. THE HERMIT

HERMES

GOD OF TRAVEL, TRADE, HOSPITALITY,
COMMUNICATION, CUNNING AND THIEVES

One of the 12 Olympians, Hermes was the official herald and messenger to the gods. He moved freely throughout all realms, and was a conductor of the dead to Hades and a protector of travellers. From birth he became a divine trickster, using wit and wile to achieve his goals.

RISEN

CONTEMPLATION, SEARCHING FOR
TRUTH, INNER GUIDANCE, WITHDRAWAL,
INTROSPECTION, ENLIGHTENMENT

It is time to take a journey. Your passage will be guided by Hermes, the protector of travellers and roamer of all realms. This journey may be across land but should also be inwards. Draw your energy and attention to focus on the one constant in all journeys: you.

You may be at a pivotal point in your life and looking at taking a new direction. It may be time to leave behind the distractions of the outside world and take the path of self-discovery, led by inner wisdom. You could find yourself withdrawing from others for a while and take this time to gain a deeper understanding of yourself.

The Hermit may appear in your life to bring you a spiritual mentor. Although witty and bright, the goal of Hermes is instead to guide you down a path to find answers within you rather than teaching them. Be conscious of life guides to help in this role, or instead wing your own feat and take this journey alone.

FALLEN

ISOLATION, PARANOIA, LONELINESS, REJECTION

You have wandered off the path and it is time to take the hand of Hermes, who is here to guide you to your chosen destination. Perhaps you have not taken enough time for introspection and reflection, or perhaps you have taken too much. There will be some struggle to connect with your spiritual self, so journey deep within your soul as you focus on its foundations. Are you avoiding looking too far within yourself because you're afraid of what you'll find?

In this time of life you may have isolated yourself too far, so it is important to take time for yourself but also worth being mindful of other people in your circles. Sometimes the low-hanging fruit lives in the next grove over. The Hermit reversed is a big sign that there is loneliness in your life. Within a relationship this can manifest as feeling shut out or unconnected.

X. WHEEL OF FORTUNE
DEMETER
GODDESS OF AGRICULTURE, GRAIN AND THE HARVEST

Demeter, one of the 12 Olympians, provided humankind with fertile soils and the fruits of the earth. In her grief over her beloved daughter Persephone's abduction by Hades she caused the season of winter and created a great famine.

RISEN

CHANGE, CYCLES, INEVITABILITY, FATE, CHANCE, FORTUNE

Like the seasons of the year, when the Wheel of Fortune card appears it reminds you that life is always in a constant state of change as the wheel turns. Good luck will return as time passes, and just so the reverse: your current fortunes could wax or wane as the wheel moves on. As the goddess of the harvest and changing seasons, Demeter is here to remind you it is important to cherish positive moments in your life, as sometimes you cannot stop your days from maturing or the wheel spinning you to new horizons. Trust, though, that balance is a part of this cycle: if you are kind, kindness will find you in turn.

This may be a difficult time if you like control and stability, but know that sometimes things will be out of your control and you can do nothing but learn to adapt and accept change.

There could be a crucial turning point in your life at the moment, so it is important to let your intuition and Demeter guide you rather than struggling and trying to hold on to the past. This card can be an indicator of destiny, and is usually a good omen.

FALLEN

LACK OF CONTROL, BAD LUCK, UNWELCOME CHANGES, DELAYS, DISRUPTION

As with the upright Wheel of Fortune, the reverse is also a card of change. However, this time it is likely to be unwelcome. You may feel a lack of control, as though external forces are working against you. Luck has not been on your side, and you have entered the winter created by Demeter when her daughter Persephone was abducted and are waiting for spring. There are lessons to be learned here, so seek out truth, learn to be more just and take control of your destiny.

Now is the time to future proof. With your finances, this could be a good indicator to save for unexpected events. This card could also reflect a resistance to change that has been forced upon you, and you may be trying to stop things from following their natural path. Find ways to embrace release and go with the flow, adapting to change while gently steering the boat with the currents.

If you have been thrust into a time of hardship this card could be a sign from Demeter that you are finally about to break a negative cycle.

XI. JUSTICE

THEMIS

GODDESS OF DIVINE LAW AND ORDER

One of the Titan gods, Themis presided over justice and also was a prophetic goddess who watched over the ancient oracles. She was not blind; however, depictions of her being blindfolded speak to her unbiased and steadfast instructions to divine law.

RISEN

CAUSE AND EFFECT, CLARITY, TRUTH, JUSTICE, LAW, CONSEQUENCES

Themis is here to call for justice, truth and the law. She is weighing and measuring you, calling you to account for your actions. If you have acted in alignment with yourself and for the greater good she will judge you kindly, but if you have acted with dishonesty your judgement will accordingly be made fairly. Themis's appearance serves as a warning to account for your actions.

If you are currently seeking justice or are the one who has been wronged, this is a sign that it will be served. It often appears when you need to make an important choice or go in search of the truth. Make sure you have been treating your partner or peers fairly, because you will reap what you sow whatever the seed or field.

Like the scales that Themis holds, make sure to balance your life and especially in a work context. Work/life balance is important, and this is a reminder to pay attention to setting the scales right.

FALLEN

DISHONESTY, UNACCOUNTABILITY, UNFAIRNESS, INJUSTICE, CORRUPTION

Justice reversed is a warning from Themis that perhaps you have done something you know is not aligned to your morals or to the detriment of others. It could also be a warning that it is not you who has stumbled but another person, and that an act of injustice has wounded you in some form. Find ways to tip the scales back again, as taking action will give you a chance to stop you from judging yourself and move forward. Don't try to blame others or avoid consequences, for this is a time to learn from what has happened and rebalance your fortunes. If there have been lies in your life then truth and honesty provide the only way forward. No amount of additional lies will redeem the first lie.

With regard to love, this card can indicate that Themis is alerting you to deception on either party's behalf. Before you cast judgements take a moment to reflect, as this is not always the reason why the Justice card has come into your reading and instead could be a warning about something outside your relationship.

XII. THE HANGED MAN
PROMETHEUS

XII. THE HANGED MAN
PROMETHEUS
GOD OF FIRE

The Titan god Prometheus tricked Zeus into accepting lesser cuts for ritual sacrifice instead of the best. In his displeasure at the deception Zeus hid fire from mortals, only to have Prometheus steal it to return it to earth. In punishment Zeus chained Prometheus to a rock for eternity, and sent an eagle sent each day to eat Prometheus's immortal – and regenerating – liver.

RISEN

SACRIFICE, CONFINEMENT, MARTYRDOM, WAITING, CONTEMPLATION

Prometheus understands that sometimes there must be sacrifice for the greater good. His card is one that serves as a reminder that sometimes a sacrifice is necessary in order to progress, whether that be a step backward to revise the path forward or as a solution to past errors. From this enlightened path and with Prometheus guiding you, know that you can see the world differently and perhaps it is not a sacrifice at all but a natural course of action. Something in your life may need to be postponed, even if there is an urgency to act, and you must take the time to reflect when you are making critical decisions.

Certain levels of compromise or sacrifice may be needed in your relationships or a change of perspective on a situation. As in Prometheus's case the sacrifice may be for the betterment of others, but do consider the cost towards yourself. You must take care of yourself before you are able to take care of others.

FALLEN

STALLING, NEEDLESS SACRIFICE, FEAR OF SACRIFICE, APATHY, DELAYS

You may be feeling as though you are sacrificing yourself or your time while getting nothing in return, and Prometheus is here to guide you to the correct path. His punishment was severe, but he then had experience with sacrifice and consequence. If everything is still on hold despite your efforts, perhaps it's time to surrender to the flow and find ways to compromise and redirect your energy. You have the power to release yourself, so try to see things from another angle.

Take a pause in your plans to contemplate whether the end result is worth the effort. While Prometheus's harsh punishment was for the betterment of mankind, is your current situation going to bring appropriate reward to yourself and others around you? If your life has been halted for a while, Prometheus may be here to alert you that the time will soon be upon you for things to once again move forward. A breakthrough may be near and a new perspective with it.

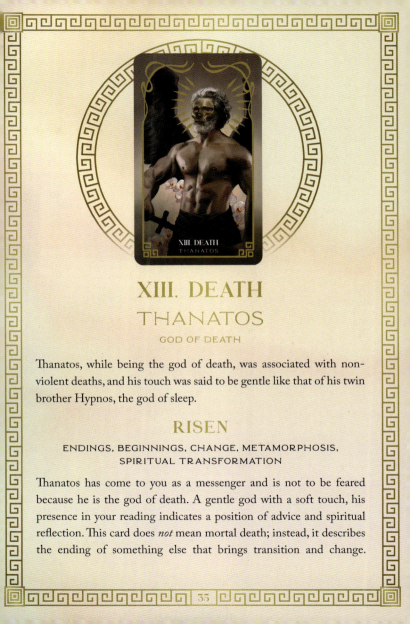

XIII. DEATH

THANATOS

GOD OF DEATH

Thanatos, while being the god of death, was associated with non-violent deaths, and his touch was said to be gentle like that of his twin brother Hypnos, the god of sleep.

RISEN

ENDINGS, BEGINNINGS, CHANGE, METAMORPHOSIS, SPIRITUAL TRANSFORMATION

Thanatos has come to you as a messenger and is not to be feared because he is the god of death. A gentle god with a soft touch, his presence in your reading indicates a position of advice and spiritual reflection. This card does *not* mean mortal death; instead, it describes the ending of something else that brings transition and change.

This should be welcomed as a positive, cleansing and transformational force in your life. The change may be sudden, unexpected, unwanted and painful, but you could find it brings a series of unanticipated opportunities and surprises for you. You may be clinging on to old patterns that are no longer serving you, so this card could be an indication it is time to move on.

Pass any old memories and baggage on to Thanatos to peacefully carry away, leaving your path clear for a fresh beginning. A new era is on its way in your life, love or career, and it's time to embrace it with open arms.

FALLEN

FEAR OF CHANGE, HOLDING ON, STAGNATION, DECAY

As with the risen position, Thanatos is communicating to you as a messenger and this card does not signal mortal death. His touch is gentle, and this softness is an indicator that you should be gentle on yourself. Thanatos's presence is not to be feared, although it does carry a message that you are resisting meaningful change and holding on to baggage and the past. You may be feeling as though you are in limbo and uncertain about the path ahead due to your inability to move forward with the weight of past beliefs holding you back. Take time to assess ways in which you may have been approaching changes in your life and whether you have been holding yourself back from something bigger. When you learn to let go of the past and embrace the present a brighter future may present itself.

Thanatos's presence can be a timely reminder to help you move forward without regret.

XIV. TEMPERANCE

ARTEMIS

GODDESS OF THE HUNT, WILDERNESS, ANIMALS AND THE MOON

Artemis was one of the 12 Olympian gods, twin sister to Apollo and a favourite goddess of the Grecian people. She was a skilled hunter who enjoyed the company of nymphs, animals and other companions. She also fiercely protected animals and the forest, punishing those who upset the balance.

RISEN

MIDDLE PATH, PATIENCE, FINDING MEANING, MODERATION, PURPOSE, HARMONY

Take a moment to breathe in Artemis's calming presence, as her appearance in your life will help you to reach for balance, patience and moderation. If things have felt stressful or frantic, let her guiding light and steady aim help you find the middle path and the tranquillity it brings. Artemis understood that finding balance was the key to harmony, not only while she was hunting but also while she was making sure to protect the game. Extremity is to be avoided, as you have the inner strength you need to remain patient and calm.

Within your relationships balance is also a key theme for this time in your life, so ensure you have a clear mind and calm heart within love. Now is a good time to work on co-operative projects, bringing together diverse groups of people or things to find the right mix of talents, experiences and abilities.

FALLEN

EXTREMES, EXCESS, LACK OF BALANCE, REALIGNMENT, HASTINESS

Artemis is here to remind you of moderation in all things *except* moderation. If you have been overindulging in unhealthy habits, engaging in negative thought patterns or overspending, now is the time to tell yourself that moderation is the key to finding balance. This card is a good reminder to connect with your body and listen to what it is telling you, finding harmony in health and happiness.

Like the constant squabbles between the gods at Olympus, you too could find there is a lack of harmony with those in your life and that you are clashing with them. Seek out your inner balance so you are more open to finding solutions together and not taking any constructive criticism harshly. Artemis's appearance in your reading can also be a warning that you're not listening to your intuition, so take some time for self-evaluation to make sure that all is well with the path you are currently taking.

XV. THE DEVIL
HADES

XV. THE DEVIL

HADES

(HAIDES) GOD OF THE UNDERWORLD

Hades was the god of the underworld and king of the dead, ruling his domain with his wife Persephone. Alongside him in the underworld was the three-headed watchdog Cerberus, and his realm consisted of multiple levels including places for the pure, heroic and wicked and those in between.

RISEN

SHADOW SELF, ATTACHMENT, RESTRICTION, SEXUALITY, SECRECY, OBSESSION, EXCESS

Hades, the god of the dead, highlights your shadow self and the negative forces that have been in play in your life. You are being held back from displaying your best self and are being ruled by your darker side and tricked into thinking you have no control over it. Both the wicked and the kind lived in the underworld ruled by Hades, and judgement is fair and just. This card is an opportunity to loosen the grip of negative patterns that have been ruling your life and seek a way back to your highest self. This may take time, so let Hades's iron-fast immovability be the anchor you place your back to and move once again into the light.

This card can represent sexuality and your wild side, with lust and temptation at the forefront of your desire for gratification. Take a moment to make sure you are opening up strong communication; Hades's treatment of his to-be wife Persephone is a lesson to learn from.

FALLEN

RELEASING, LIMITING BELIEFS, EXPLORING DARKNESS, DETACHMENT, FREEDOM, REVELATION, INDEPENDENCE

Things may be holding you back at the moment, but Hades is one of the three rulers of the cosmos so take on his power and strength to break the chains that are tethering you to your unhealthy attachments or beliefs. Now is the time to smash harmful habits and find the strength to overcome addiction. You may be entering your own personal underworld, exploring and journeying into your innermost shadows. If you are doing this consciously you can embody Hades's strength and release those shadows or find ways to accept and embrace them in a constructive way in your life. If this path was taken unwillingly and you have entered a period of thinking darkly, it is time to reach out to those around you or seek out someone trained to help you work through this time.

This card is a signal that you have the strength to break free from a toxic friendship or relationship, enabling you to enter a phase of having more control over your independence.

XVI. THE TOWER

POSEIDON

GOD OF THE SEA, WATER, EARTHQUAKES AND HORSES

Poseidon, one of the 12 Olympians, ruled earth alongside Hades and Zeus. His domain to rule was the sea, and he had a special affinity with horses. He was also connected with the land and was the cause of earthquakes.

RISEN

SUDDEN UPHEAVAL, BROKEN PRIDE, DISASTER, TRAUMA, CHAOS

Like a crashing, turbulent sea and the brutal chaos of an earthquake, Poseidon has entered your reading to warn you of change in the most radical and momentous way. This does not have to be an ominous prediction, however, as change is a normal part of life. You may need to question long-held beliefs and be as flexible and ever-moving as the ocean, finding fresh processes and ways of thinking. Take on the strength of Poseidon to make sure you grow from this, becoming stronger, wiser and more resilient with a new perspective on life.

As with the arguments between Poseidon and some of his Olympian siblings, he serves as a warning towards an inevitable argument to come. Try to keep your temper in check at work and with those you love: open up communication as much as possible and be prepared to take steps to fix things. Strong foundations in your relationship will be key to weathering the storm.

FALLEN

DISASTER AVOIDED OR DELAYED, FEAR OF SUFFERING, RESISTING CHANGE

Instead of being subjected to rough seas and earthquakes on the land above, you are experiencing strong rip currents and turbulence in the ocean's depths below. Poseidon in the fallen position suggests you are undergoing a large personal transformation and upheaval, as opposed to one caused by external circumstances. You may be going through an existential crisis or having your belief systems, purpose and values questioned. Like trying to fight the current, you may be resisting this change and delaying the inevitable upheaval or clinging on to your old beliefs. It is time to take Poseidon's hand and let the current direct you, taking it on board as growth and transformation.

This may also be a sign of a disaster narrowly avoided, and you need to learn the lesson to prevent being wiped out by the next wave. If there are things you know need to come to a close but you are delaying due to the pain it will bring, this card may give you the strength you need to enact change: either letting it go with the current to move on or making extreme adjustments so you can move forward.

XVII. THE STAR

NYX

GODDESS OF THE NIGHT

Nyx was one of the primordial gods, emerging from chaos at the beginning of creation. Coupling with the god of darkness Erebus, she became mother to many of the primordial deities and was feared even by Zeus.

RISEN

HOPE, FAITH, RENEWAL, REJUVENATION, PURPOSE, SERENITY

Nyx's bright stars shine light through the darkness you have experienced to bring a calm serenity to your life. You have suffered from loss, but the stars are coming out from the night sky and searching within to shine on your resilience and inner power.

No matter what is hurled your way you can affirm your sense of self and allow yourself to dream of striving to reach the stars.

You may find in this period of life you are searching out the highest and most authentic version of yourself. In this positive and changed period of your life there are suggestions of a generous spirit and a wish to share this new emotional wealth with others to give back to those you care for. You may be experiencing a new sense of creativity, so harness this by exploring any new hobbies you have been considering.

If you are seeking relationships, the light shining from you makes this a great time to meet people. If you're already in a relationship then channelling the deep synergy between Nyx and her partner Erebus will help strengthen your own, which is a sign that you may be progressing to something deeper.

FALLEN

FAITHLESSNESS, DISCOURAGEMENT, INSECURITY, DESPAIR, DISCONNECTION, MONOTONY

The night sky is dark and Nyx is throwing darkness upon you when The Star card is reversed in your reading. Faith and hope may have dimmed: things are dark, and there are few stars in the sky to shine the way forward. You are currently going through a test of faith, so you must reaffirm your conviction and have confidence in yourself.

If you're feeling disconnected and overwhelmed, find ways to reconnect with what is most important to you and listen to what the chorus of your soul is whispering. If you need help, seek out support. This is a good time to rediscover your creative side, leaning on it to help you heal. If you're picking at your own flaws or feeling unworthy of love at the moment, Nyx in your life is a reminder to take some time to once again fall deeply in love with yourself.

XVIII. THE MOON

SELENE

GODDESS OF THE MOON

Sister to the god of the sun Helios and the goddess of the dawn Eos, Selene was the personification of and Titan goddess of the moon. While multiple other goddesses were associated with the moon, Selene was frequently represented as being the moon incarnate.

RISEN

ILLUSIONS, INTUITION, COMPLEXITY, SECRETS, ANXIETY

When Selene appears in the sky she signals that all is not as it seems. Fears and illusions may be clouding your vision at the moment, leaving you in a time of uncertainty. When this card appears in your reading be wary, as you may find out later that you only have half the information needed and hasty decisions may be your downfall. Listen to your intuition and allow Selene's serenity to lead you to higher levels of understanding. She may be present in your dreams, communicating with your powerful unconscious mind.

In a relationship, things may look happy to the outside world but Selene's moonlight will highlight the imperfections. This is an opportunity to grow, as Selene herself did. Try to open up stronger communication to make sure no information has been missed and that nuance and intention are understood. If you are single, be wary of potential deceit or a misunderstanding with others or with yourself.

FALLEN

RELEASING FEAR, UNVEILING, TRUTH, BLOCKED INTUITION

As Selene falls lower in the sky she brings a release of fears and anxiety. Entreat her to assist you in energy clearing, as she is a willing partner who may provide it to help you find clarity. In general, you will feel a lifting of energy as light begins to return to your sky and life begins to feel a little more stable after previous turmoil. Make efforts to identify and address your fears and anxieties, reaching out for support if necessary.

As you enter the dark side of the moon and are creatively inclined you may feel a block in place that may blur the lines between reality and fantasy, especially if supporting cards are negative. Selene's final beams of moonlight will shine light upon lies, unveiling them. Within love this can be the truth of your relationship coming to light. It can also be external deception or a lifting of any deceptions you may be telling yourself about how you feel towards someone.

XIX. THE SUN

HELIOS

GOD OF THE SUN

Helios was the original Titan sun god, riding his chariot across the sky to bring sunlight to the world before this became Apollo's domain.

RISEN

VITALITY, JOY, WARMTH, CONFIDENCE, TRUTH, POSITIVITY

Helios, the personification of and god of the sun, brings radiance and abundance to give you strength and positive energy when this card is in your reading. This beautiful energy radiating from you will help you overcome challenges and bring warmth into the lives of the people around you. You may be experiencing a boost in positivity and vitality, harnessing this to a wonderful sense of health and energy.

Make sure to take the opportunity to harness Helios's power to shine your love on the people you care about.

For your relationships, this can arrive as a period of passion and fun. It can also highlight any issues by either bringing them into the light to solve and grow from or, in some cases, bringing an end to pave the way for something new. The Sun is a card of truth, and opening up to Helios will help shine a light on any deceit or lies you may have been a victim of.

FALLEN

NEGATIVITY, DEPRESSION, SADNESS, OPPRESSION, CONCEITEDNESS, EXCESSIVE ENTHUSIASM

With the sun reversed and Helios's light absent you may notice darkness in your life, that you are getting weighed down by things that are happening around you. Remind yourself to find time in the sunlight and stay present, putting your worries and concerns to the side as you take a moment to lighten your heart and become mindful. This card is a reminder to search your inner self to see what might have led you to experience setbacks or dampened your enthusiasm and optimism. It strives to make you aware that many obstacles only exist in your mind and many more can only be removed with the right mindset.

Alternatively, this could be a warning that Helios and the sun are shining too bright in your life and you've become too overconfident and optimistic. It's a reminder to check your ego and make sure that what you've set out to achieve is realistic.

XX. JUDGEMENT

ATHENA

(PALLAS ATHENA, ATHENE) GODDESS OF WISDOM, BATTLE STRATEGY AND REASON

One of the most famous and beloved goddesses of the Grecian people and one of the 12 Olympians, Athena was a fierce armed warrior goddess so her aid was often synonymous with military prowess. Her wisdom and reason were well respected and her council often sought after by gods and mortals. She could be swift with her judgement and harsh in retribution, her treatment of Medusa being a prime example: it was Athena who turned Medusa's hair into snakes.

RISEN

SWIFT JUDGEMENT, RECKONING, DECISIVENESS, REFLECTION, AWAKENING

Seek Athena's council if you reach a significant point in your life where you must step back and evaluate yourself. You have entered a time of awakening, when issues you have previously ignored may now be seen clearly. When you take on Athena's wisdom and reason you can achieve a level of composure and clarity that will help you assess yourself and your choices to ensure positive outcomes. A big decision may have arrived in your life, and it is of great import to have acted honourably and truthfully for a resolved outcome. If you have acted in bad faith it is time to clear your conscience and atone for misdeeds, releasing guilt or sadness. As you reach this crossroads in your journey you may find comfort in sharing your struggles with others, so support each other and rise together.

Within relationships, you may find yourself being the one doing the judging. It is important to forgive past mistakes and talk through feelings without apportioning blame to find a solution to move forward.

FALLEN

INDECISIVENESS, UNFAIR BLAME, SELF-LOATHING, DOUBT, LACK OF SELF-AWARENESS

Athena's gaze weighs heavily upon you and has been reflected in your self-judgment. Fear and self-doubt may be holding you back from moving forward and taking the path needed for positive direction. Focusing on past mistakes can sometimes blind you from taking much-needed lessons from those mistakes, so take the time and space to consider without harsh judgement. Through working on your own self-acceptance, self-love and acceptance of others you can find release and the freedom to fulfil your true potential.

Athena's call is inviting you to something bigger, and it is time to pay attention.

In relationships, learn from Athena's own hasty judgements and unjust punishments of various Grecian women. Take the time to gather all of the facts before racing to an interpretation of the behaviour of others. Holding on to negativity will disable you from moving forward within your relationships. Ensure that any critique provided is productive and fair.

XXI. THE WORLD

GAEA

(GAIA, GE) MOTHER OF ALL, THE FIRST GODDESS

Gaea, who was born from chaos, was one of the first primordial deities. She mothered the first Titan gods, including the Gigantes and mortal creatures, and personified earth. Gaea created her own husband, Uranus, to be her companion, though it was a marriage of hardships. Her great love for her children later assisted her in overthrowing him.

RISEN

WHOLENESS, HARMONY, COMPLETION, ACCOMPLISHMENT, SUCCESS, BELONGING, TRAVEL

After hardships endured and lessons learned, with The World card within your reading and Gaea guiding you it is time to reap the rewards from the seeds you have sown. Loose ends need to be tied up or cut away. Mother Earth appearing means the world is at your fingertips, which could be in a literal sense as The World is one of the travel cards. You may meet someone new while travelling or someone who brings travel into your life. It is also a good time to stop and reflect upon universal and global awareness, and to appreciate people and cultures from across the world and your place within that tapestry.

As with Gaea's creations of the earth and her beloved children, take pride in what you have achieved; it hasn't been easy to get here, but you have endured and made it. Perhaps you have realised a dream or completed a challenge, so make sure to stop and savor the moment. Sharing the fruits of your hard work with the people who helped you along the way may prove its own reward.

This card can also represent reaching your career goals, and financial stability or rewards. Learn from Gaea's mistakes in her failed attempts to overthrow Zeus from power, and understand that now is not the time for risky gambles.

FALLEN

STAGNATION, LACK OF SUCCESS, LACK OF COMPLETION, FEELING INCOMPLETE, BURDENS

As Gaea is turned away from you, you may have found things have become stagnant and you have not accomplished what you set out to do. This may be because you tried to take shortcuts, pouring energy into fruitless ventures. It is time to step back, accept and embrace where you are now, let go of the past and move on in your personal journey. If you're near the end of a project or goal maintain focus; you only have a short way to go, thus it's important to re-energise and be creative in solutions so you can enjoy the pleasures of completion. You may be struggling to move on from an unexpected ending to a relationship in your life or letting past events colour your current relationship, so it is time to tie up loose ends, without getting knotted, to find joy and love in the now.

Make sure to keep your heart and self open for Mother Earth's healing to find peace and move on to happiness.

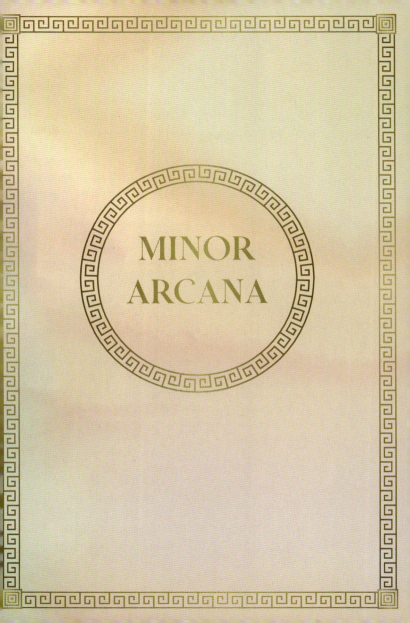

MINOR

ARCANA

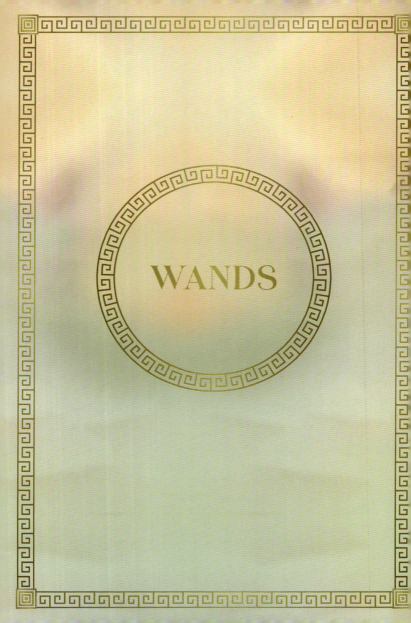

WANDS

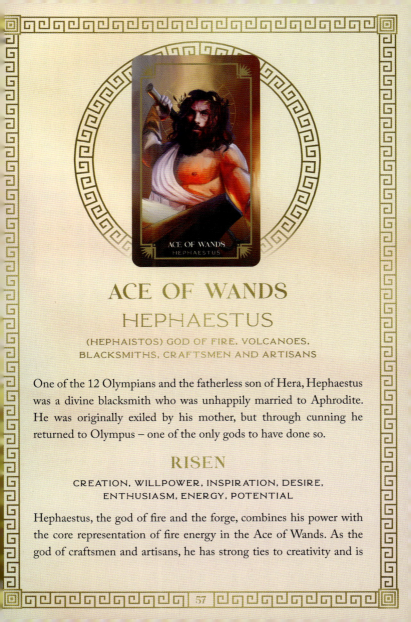

ACE OF WANDS

HEPHAESTUS

(HEPHAISTOS) GOD OF FIRE, VOLCANOES, BLACKSMITHS, CRAFTSMEN AND ARTISANS

One of the 12 Olympians and the fatherless son of Hera, Hephaestus was a divine blacksmith who was unhappily married to Aphrodite. He was originally exiled by his mother, but through cunning he returned to Olympus – one of the only gods to have done so.

RISEN

CREATION, WILLPOWER, INSPIRATION, DESIRE, ENTHUSIASM, ENERGY, POTENTIAL

Hephaestus, the god of fire and the forge, combines his power with the core representation of fire energy in the Ace of Wands. As the god of craftsmen and artisans, he has strong ties to creativity and is here to help you release yours. Creativity comes in more forms than just art: it can represent a place in which you find your own vision and voice. This is the time for taking a chance and pursuing an idea you have in mind, for following your instincts. Keep in mind, though, that while Hephaestus is encouraging you to pursue your potential the results are not guaranteed. You need more than a spark to keep flames burning.

FALLEN

LACK OF DIRECTION, PROCRASTINATION, CREATIVE BLOCKS, DELAYS, HESITANCY

With Hephaestus in the fallen position, the flames of the forge are banked and you may be feeling uninspired or unmotivated. If you have a goal in mind, you may not be feeling excited to achieve it. There may be delays, or a hesitancy on how to complete it. Take your time and have patience as the fire is stoked – passion will return with time.

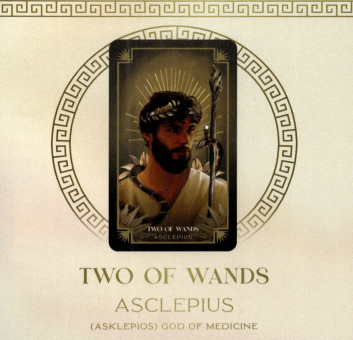

TWO OF WANDS

ASCLEPIUS

(ASKLEPIOS) GOD OF MEDICINE

A favoured son of Apollo, Asclepius was taught medicine by his father and the centaur Chiron. He became so skilled he could bring back the dead, and Zeus punished this crime against natural order by destroying Asclepius with a thunderbolt. He was placed among the stars as the constellation Ophiuchus. His staff is today's symbol of modern medicine and is often mistaken for the similar caduceus of Hermes.

RISEN

PLANNING, MAKING DECISIONS, DISCOVERY, PROGRESS

Asclepius and his intense desire to learn and unparalleled skills in his field are here to help you with your own skills. You are undergoing a period of progression, and while you have all the potential you need to achieve what you've set out to do you just need a little nudge. You may be experiencing a choice, an intersection of some sort.

As with Asclepius's apprenticeship with Chiron, you may have further education or travel in mind to help with your long-term future. You can achieve amazing things, and now is the time to put them into action. What has to happen to get you where you need to be?

FALLEN

FEAR OF CHANGE, PLAYING SAFE, BAD PLANNING

As there are lessons from the gods' incredible successes, there are also warnings to be heeded from their downfall. From overconfidence or a lack of patience you may have ignored some of the finer details with your future planning, which has ultimately led to an undesirable outcome. Reconnect with your vision, making sure it is in line with your values, and consider exploring new options to actualise it. The hardest paths sometimes lead to the most rewarding pastures.

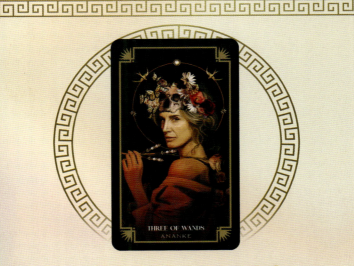

THREE OF WANDS

ANANKE

GODDESS OF INEVITABILITY, COMPULSION AND NECESSITY

Ananke was a primordial goddess who was self-formed at the dawn of creation. As the mother of the Moirai, or the Fates, she was the only one who could control their actions and therefore direct the fate of all gods and mortals.

RISEN

LOOKING AHEAD, EXPANSION, TRAVEL, FORESIGHT, PROGRESS

The goddess of inevitability and necessity, Ananke's presence tells of the march of time to the future. Look ahead and see the horizon and the paths that lead to it – and beyond. Ananke's presence will broaden your vision so you understand the various points of no return, and consequently help you take steps to avoid fruitless pursuits. Her presence may also indicate travel, foreign lands and concepts. Some situations are unavoidable, so consider preparing for them ahead of time. Serene searching will set up a soul that can synergise with success.

FALLEN

OBSTACLES, DELAYS, LACK OF FORESIGHT, RESTRICTION

Ananke's gaze is upon you, and she has no flexibility for any god or mortal; inevitable fate marches on. Now may be a time to step back and look at the paths ahead before it is too late, thus avoiding situations that arise from obstacles you cannot readily equal. If you have a task to complete perhaps you should review your understanding, goals, contingencies and time keeping.

Ananke is a reminder to plan for the future and act with deliberation and care.

FOUR OF WANDS

HESTIA

GODDESS OF THE HEARTH, DOMESTICITY, FAMILY AND FIRE

Once one of the 12 Olympians, Hestia left Olympus and Dionysus took her place. She swore to remain a maiden forever and presides over domestic life and the family hearth.

RISEN

COMMUNITY, HOME, CELEBRATION, SUCCESS, ACHIEVEMENTS, FAMILY

Hestia, as goddess of the hearth and family, has come at a time for the sharing of connection and celebration with those you love the most. This could be with or without a special occasion; it is merely a reminder to spend quality time with friends and family.

It is important to take the time to show those around you what they mean to you and let yourself recognise feelings of support and happiness when they surround you.

Hestia could be indicating there is an unexpected celebration coming in the future such as the completion of an important milestone or the creation of something new.

FALLEN

LACK OF SUPPORT, TRANSIENCE, HOME CONFLICTS, INSTABILITY, SELF-DOUBT

In the fallen position Hestia's presence is a flickering ember in the family hearth. Discord may be present in your home and chosen family, which you may be experiencing through a lack of support such as completing something important only to find an indifferent reaction when you expected celebration. Communication and honesty without accusations are key here: take on Hestia's warm flame so you can express your feelings in a constructive way in order to strengthen ties once more.

Instead of with those in your chosen family circle you may instead be experiencing disruption from a stage of life in which you feel little stability and security, such as moving home or your job or mindset.

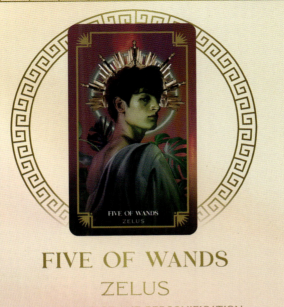

FIVE OF WANDS

ZELUS

(ZELOS) GOD OF AND PERSONIFICATION OF RIVALRY AND ENVY

Zelus was the son of the infernal River Styx and a brother to the goddess of victory Nike, the god of strength Kratos and the goddess of force Bia. Zelus was a winged enforcer of Zeus's court.

RISEN

COMPETITION, RIVALRY, CONFLICT, JEALOUSY, ENVY, COMMUNICATION BREAKDOWN

Zelus, the god of rivalry and envy, presents a warning of conflict. You may be in the middle of competition with others, and rather than working towards a common goal tension is hampering your ability to move forward. There might have been a breakdown of communication, with more speaking than hearing. Know that diversity of opinion should be encouraged as it presents an opportunity to learn from differences.

You may be experiencing feelings of jealousy, though Zelus is warning you this is a time to accept competition as a way of improving yourself, letting go of feelings of malice towards the subject of your envy.

FALLEN

AVOIDING CONFLICT, RESPECTING DIFFERENCES, DISAGREEMENTS, COMPROMISE

With Zelus in the fallen position and gazing away from you, you may find peace within yourself. Perhaps you find yourself in a break after a period of competition and conflict, having reached a compromise that suits all parties involved. In the checks and balances of life there is also a place for the god of rivalry. You may be avoiding conflict at the moment, deflecting issues and failing to assert your point of view. It is important to reflect on whether you are compromising on something important to you, because in order to stay true to your values sometimes conflict is needed. It is best to find a way of ensuring conflict is engaged in constructively.

SIX OF WANDS

NIKE

GODDESS OF VICTORY

A daughter of the infernal River Styx and a sister to the god of rivalry Zelus, the god of strength Kratos and the goddess of force Bia, Nike was often connected with Athena and Zeus and her victory is presiding over all things, not just war.

RISEN

VICTORY, SUCCESS, PUBLIC REWARD, STABILITY, PRIDE, SHARED ACHIEVEMENTS

The goddess of victory is here to congratulate you: you may be close to or have already attained an important milestone or achievement, something that may be significant only to you. Singing your accolades, Nike is a sign to be proud of what you achieved, to believe in yourself and your accomplishments so far. You may have received public acknowledgement for your achievements or will soon. Nike's presence is very positive for work and career goals and is a good omen.

It is time to share the spotlight, so if you are in a relationship you will likely lift each other up and achieve your goals together.

FALLEN

LACK OF RECOGNITION, DIFFERENCES, CRITICISM, FAILURE, EXCESS PRIDE, VULNERABILITY

Victory and the feeling of success is not currently with you, and you may feel the absence of Nike by your side. You might be navigating negative terrain, doubting your abilities and overall potential. Perhaps your current efforts have been met with criticism instead of accolades, leaving you feeling flat. As Nike was a companion to Athena, what you may need is a close friend or third party to pick you up and provide support, encouragement and strength to help you achieve the innate potential you have inside you.

SEVEN OF WANDS

SOTERIA

GODDESS OF SAFETY, SALVATION AND DELIVERANCE

A mysterious figure in the lore of the gods, Soteria was the goddess of safety and preservation from harm, her name being invoked as a sanctuary.

RISEN

PERSEVERANCE, DEFENSIVENESS, MAINTAINING CONTROL, SETTING BOUNDARIES, CHALLENGE

You may be finding unexpected competition in your life, that perhaps you are the subject of another person's envy. Soteria, the goddess of safety and salvation, is here for an extra layer of protection against those who wish to challenge you. Find sanctuary within her calming arms because she knows you have the stamina and strength to withhold, endure and overcome and is here to lend her own defensive strength. This is a sign to hold your ground and stay true to your beliefs and what you value most.

FALLEN

GIVING UP, DESTROYED CONFIDENCE, BEING OVERWHELMED, EXHAUSTION, BURNOUT

Soteria's arms encircle you both in the risen and fallen position and you may really need her protection right now. You are perhaps being weighed down by external pressure that is beginning to leave you exhausted. Stay firm! This is your reminder to remain the truest version of yourself and not compromise your values. Take from Soteria her protective energy, drawing strength from it and approaching your situation with courage. Be wary to avoid too much aggression: like a dog backed in to a corner, when upset and tired you may bite someone you care about by accident.

EIGHT OF WANDS

ATALANTA

MORTAL HEROINE RENOWNED FOR HER RUNNING

Although Atalanta was not a goddess her running skills landed her among legends, and as a strong woman in a patriarchal world as a legacy to be celebrated. She was a swift-footed huntress who was as skilled as men in hunting and faster than all. She was tricked into losing a race with some golden apples and therefore into marriage with a slower man by Aphrodite.

RISEN

RAPID ACTION, MOVEMENT, QUICK DECISIONS, INSPIRATION

There is a strong energy in your life that is propelling you forward, and you move like the great heroine Atalanta in all her speed and skill. While not a goddess and unable to lend her power, she was such an inspirational force that you can find the same strength within yourself to keep your footing steady through this fast momentum. Whatever you turn yourself to will take off at tremendous speed, so it is time to utilise this force. You may be very busy, but it's the good kind of busy that keeps you enthusiastic and happy at the progress you're making.

Be careful of being swept off your feet by someone in your life. It could be a whirlwind holiday romance or a strong connection that takes off quickly.

FALLEN

PANIC, WAITING, SLOWING DOWN, DISTRACTIONS, BEING OUT OF CONTROL, IMPATIENCE

If this card is in the fallen position you may be imbued with a fast pace but perhaps you are charging ahead too fast. You could miss something in your haste, leading to mistakes.

At the moment there is no middle ground: either you're racing forward too fast and at risk of tripping over your own feet or you feel as though you're at a standstill and things are progressing too slowly. Don't be distracted by the golden apples thrown at your feet; keep looking for alternate paths around the challenges that are presented to find completion of your plans. If it is too distracting and the terrain too rough, hold off for a short time until things become more stable.

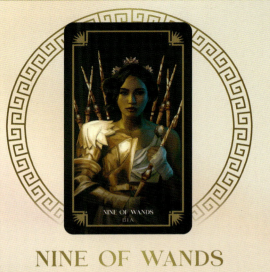

NINE OF WANDS

BIA

GODDESS OF AND PERSONIFICATION OF FORCE

A daughter of the infernal River Styx and a sister to the goddess of victory Nike, the god of strength Kratos and the god of envy Zelus, Bia was also an enforcer of Zeus's court, having helped him overthrow his father to become the king of the gods.

RISEN

RESILIENCE, GRIT, LAST STAND, PERSISTENCE, HOPE

Bia, the goddess of force, may come as a sign you are going through opposition and adversity but that you remain standing strong. You are an immovable force, taking the battering but showing an inner strength and grit that lets you grow every time an obstacle is thrown in your path. Bia is letting you know you already have everything you need to overcome this difficulty: it could be your inner strength, someone in your life who can help or something in your possession. Take this as a sign of encouragement and hope that you will overcome this.

FALLEN

EXHAUSTION, FATIGUE, QUESTIONING MOTIVATIONS

You have been strong for a while but may be feeling overcome by responsibilities and setbacks. You cannot currently feel Bia's force and strength and may feel too physically or mentally exhausted to take on new challenges. This could be a time to reach out for help, so if you cannot carry on then seek out assistance from those around you to take over some of the burden. With less on your plate they can help you recoup and regain your strength and force to withstand what life throws at you. Look for a solution to deal with what life is delivering to you before it consumes you.

TEN OF WANDS

IRIS

GODDESS OF AND PERSONIFICATION OF RAINBOWS

Iris was not only the goddess and personification of rainbows but was also a messenger of the gods. Whenever a god had to take a solemn oath it was her duty to carry water from the River Styx to them.

RISEN

ACCOMPLISHMENT, RESPONSIBILITY, BURDEN, HARD WORK, COMPLETION

You feel no stranger to responsibility and with it comes a kinship with the goddess Iris, one of the messengers to the Olympian gods. Iris is a sign there is a rainbow in sight at long last, that you've finally made it to where you strived. Even with her many colours shining bright her tasks as a messenger keep her on her toes, and likewise you may feel flooded by responsibilities at the moment. Remember that Iris was not the sole messenger, and have a look to see where the workload can be shared. Make sure to enjoy the fruits of your labour and see beauty in the world around you.

FALLEN

INABILITY TO DELEGATE, OVERSTRESSED, BURNED OUT, RELEASE, MARTYRDOM

As with Iris in the risen position, the Ten of Wands appearing fallen is a reminder that success often comes with responsibility and a high workload. You're trying to take on everything yourself and all of a sudden you are drowning beneath the load. Reach out to your friends and family; you don't have to do it alone. Iris was not the only messenger goddess, and those around you can help.

Have a look at what is causing you distress and ask yourself whether it is truly causing a positive impact on what you value or instead dimming the bright colours in your sky. If it is, maybe it's time to let it go.

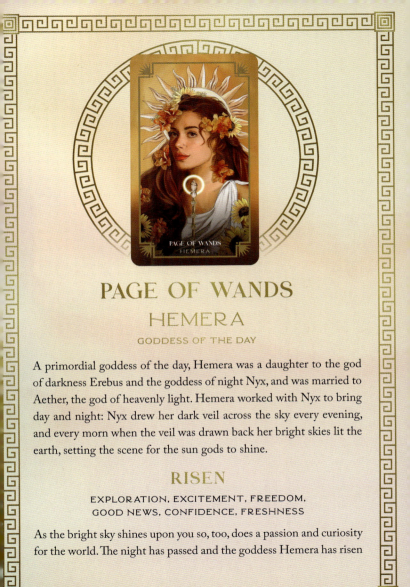

PAGE OF WANDS

HEMERA

GODDESS OF THE DAY

A primordial goddess of the day, Hemera was a daughter to the god
of darkness Erebus and the goddess of night Nyx, and was married to
Aether, the god of heavenly light. Hemera worked with Nyx to bring
day and night: Nyx drew her dark veil across the sky every evening,
and every morn when the veil was drawn back her bright skies lit the
earth, setting the scene for the sun gods to shine.

RISEN

EXPLORATION, EXCITEMENT, FREEDOM,
GOOD NEWS, CONFIDENCE, FRESHNESS

As the bright sky shines upon you so, too, does a passion and curiosity
for the world. The night has passed and the goddess Hemera has risen

to bring energy and opportunities in the light of day. Now is the time to embrace new journeys and projects to see where they take you. Let this trigger courage within you to overcome personal doubts so you can boldly move forward.

FALLEN

LACK OF DIRECTION, PROCRASTINATION, CREATING CONFLICT

Hemera's light is blinding you, and the potential of the day ahead has left you paralysed by choices between too many pathways and plans. Perhaps you've been unable to follow anything past the planning stage or have started hobbies and projects only to find they end up nowhere. Let the light of Hemera shine on fresh pathways for you to follow; perhaps a different approach may help you to reconnect with your original vision or take another direction entirely.

The day will always return after the night, and you have time to play with ideas that may eventually grow.

KNIGHT OF WANDS

HERACLES

(HERAKLES, HERCULES, ALCAEUS, ALCIDES) DIVINE HERO

Born a mortal, Heracles was the son of Zeus and was a constant victim of Hera's jealous machinations. He completed a number of heroic quests and feats of strength and skill that eventually resulted in his death through treachery. His actions were so notable in life that the divine part of his essence ascended to the heavens, becoming a god and marrying the goddess Hebe.

RISEN

ACTION, ADVENTURE, FEARLESSNESS, HASTE, EXCITEMENT, RISK-TAKING

When the bold, adventurous and strong Heracles turns up in your hand it is no wonder you are filled with a confidence and desire for adventure. You know that growth and expansion wait on the other side and it is time to take calculated risks to complete new goals. This card indicates a good time to travel and full health. There may be a warning about haste, so it is important to take things at a pace by which you are able to think things through and achieve your goals without injury or complications.

FALLEN

ANGER, IMPULSIVENESS, RECKLESSNESS, DELAYS, FRUSTRATIONS

You may be channelling the struggles and trials that Hera threw at Heracles, such as experiencing setbacks and delays that culminate in a feeling of frustration at the lack of movement. You are still filled with power and energy, but it has nowhere to go. Check yourself by giving space and time before any action, ensuring that you do not do or say something through impulsivity that you later regret.

You or someone in your life may be running from the idea of commitment or experiencing changes of heart, and thus leaving others confused.

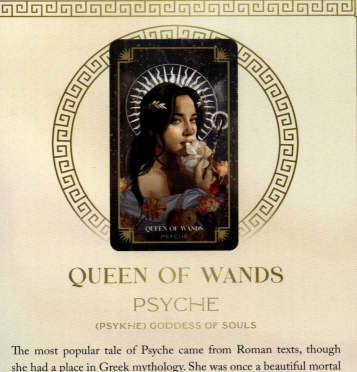

QUEEN OF WANDS

PSYCHE

(PSYKHE) GODDESS OF SOULS

The most popular tale of Psyche came from Roman texts, though she had a place in Greek mythology. She was once a beautiful mortal princess who earned the ire of Aphrodite and the love of her son Eros, and she was eventually transformed after many trials into a goddess and married him.

RISEN

COURAGE, DETERMINATION, JOY, OPTIMISM, CHARISMA

Though in initial appearances Psyche was just a beautiful mortal woman, her grit, passion and focus were all revealed when she set out to accomplish all the trials Aphrodite threw at her. She is here to remind you that you too are courageous, determined and able to follow through with your visions, even in the face of adversity and challenge.

Be bold in your undertakings and let yourself shine brightly; you may accomplish a significant amount in a short time. As a mortal who managed to capture the heart of the god of love, Psyche is also here to celebrate your independent, self-assured and optimistic sides, bringing you a confidence and charisma that may ultimately draw people to you who resonate with your highest self.

FALLEN

SELFISHNESS, INSECURITY, BURNOUT, BEING OVERWHELMED, LOW CONFIDENCE

Even with Psyche turned from you her power to call forward your soul is still strong. This is a calling to bring your energy and attention inward to rebuild by accessing your personal strengths and inner voice. It is a call to truly look at discovering who you are and to be courageous in expressing it. As with the hubris that called down Aphrodite's wrath on Psyche, you should reflect on whether you are being self-centred rather than self-assured. You may find you need to take some time out as you may be wrestling with too much and heading for burnout.

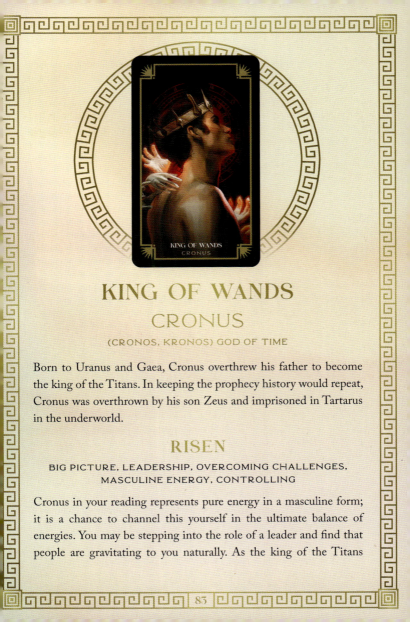

KING OF WANDS

CRONUS

(CRONOS, KRONOS) GOD OF TIME

Born to Uranus and Gaea, Cronus overthrew his father to become the king of the Titans. In keeping the prophecy history would repeat, Cronus was overthrown by his son Zeus and imprisoned in Tartarus in the underworld.

RISEN

BIG PICTURE, LEADERSHIP, OVERCOMING CHALLENGES, MASCULINE ENERGY, CONTROLLING

Cronus in your reading represents pure energy in a masculine form; it is a chance to channel this yourself in the ultimate balance of energies. You may be stepping into the role of a leader and find that people are gravitating to you naturally. As the king of the Titans

Cronus understood delegation, and you may feel yourself being in charge of the larger vision with the people around you doing the work. Take heed from Cronus's final fate: you may hold the power at the moment, but if it is abused or coveted there will be consequences.

FALLEN

IMPULSIVENESS, OVERBEARING, HIGH EXPECTATIONS, CONTROLLING, INSECURITY, POWERLESSNESS

When Cronos is turned from you his aggression and arrogance in pursuing power may be playing a factor in your life via unbalanced masculine energies. On one hand you may have too much, channelling his arrogance, control and stubbornness, so step back and see how you are interacting with others and make sure you are not taking for granted someone's good intentions and efforts for you. Alternatively, you may find that power has gone the other way and the masculine energy you hold has taken a back seat, so take a proactive approach and reconnect with your inner potency and confidence.

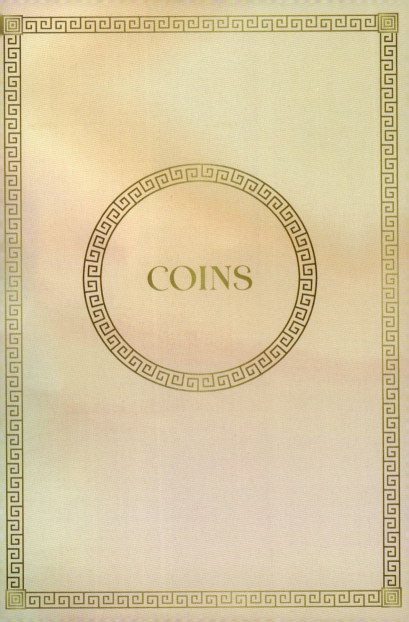

COINS

ACE OF COINS

AEOLUS

(AIOLOS) KEEPER OF THE WINDS

Aeolus, as noted in the Odyssey, was the keeper of the winds, with the power to still and rouse winds blessed upon him by Zeus. He kept the violent storm winds locked away on his isle, waiting for only the greatest god's command to release them.

RISEN

OPPORTUNITY, PROSPERITY, NEW VENTURE, ABUNDANCE, STABILITY, NEW HORIZONS

Like a fresh breeze from a different direction, this card represents new beginnings and prosperity. Aeolus opened the gates to let in strong winds, blowing away stagnation and leaving you open to new opportunities. This is not a free ride, and it is up to you to discern how best to steer once things begin to move. Keep your eyes open for new chances and opportunities to further your goals.

This breath of fresh air also can symbolise wealth in different aspects of your life, if not financial then in the broader sense of happiness, potential and fulfilment. Now is a good time for trying new things, leaving the old behind and following the breeze towards fresh futures.

FALLEN

LOST OPPORTUNITIES, MISSED CHANCES, BAD INVESTMENTS, INSTABILITY, SCARCITY

With Aeolus in the fallen position an ill wind is blowing. You have no control over it and may find yourself buffeted by the gale. You can see the opportunities in front of you, but when you try to grasp them you are moving in a different direction and find they have been lost. It is a time to be cautious with financial decisions and wary that perhaps what seemed like a sure thing may end up falling through if you are not careful. Try to slow down, find strength through planning and preparation and learn to ride the winds to make sure that any new ventures are as risk free as possible.

TWO OF COINS
OCEANUS
(OKEANOS) GOD OF THE RIVER OKEANOS AND OCEANS

Oceanus was the oldest Titan, a primordial god and the son of Uranus and Gaea and father to thousands of stream spirits and ocean nymphs. He was the resident god of a river of the same name.

RISEN
BALANCING DECISIONS, PRIORITIES, ADAPTABILITY, FLEXIBILITY

In the ways of the many currents of the ocean, you may be currently juggling multiple roles and priorities. As the god of personification of the ocean, Oceanus has an inherent knowledge of the focus required to orchestrate all the many currents at once. He can help you through your time of fast-moving waters even if you feel as though you are rushing from one thing to the next. You may find you can't give your loved ones the energy and time needed to keep them happy and that the balance of work and life is a hard line to walk. This card may be the reminder you need to stay flexible and adaptable, following the flow of the water and understanding that week to week different things will need your attention to stay balanced.

FALLEN

LOSS OF BALANCE, DISORGANISATION, BEING OVERWHELMED, OVEREXTENSION, REPRIORITISATION

Oceanus in reverse has a similar meaning to the risen position: you may be on an ocean ledge as you try to navigate the many pulls and currents. This time, however, you have found yourself in the rapids with things getting away from you. In struggling to stay afloat you may be ignoring other areas of your life that need attention and will ultimately be pulled in many directions. Reassess your priorities and goals and learn to live within your potential. Allow yourself the space to come up to breathe.

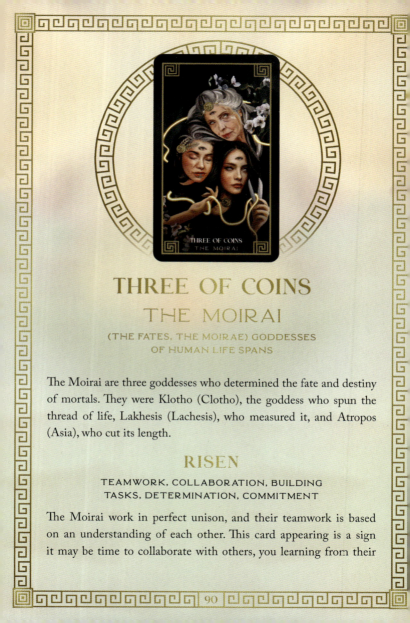

THREE OF COINS

THE MOIRAI

(THE FATES, THE MOIRAE) GODDESSES OF HUMAN LIFE SPANS

The Moirai are three goddesses who determined the fate and destiny of mortals. They were Klotho (Clotho), the goddess who spun the thread of life, Lakhesis (Lachesis), who measured it, and Atropos (Asia), who cut its length.

RISEN

TEAMWORK, COLLABORATION, BUILDING TASKS, DETERMINATION, COMMITMENT

The Moirai work in perfect unison, and their teamwork is based on an understanding of each other. This card appearing is a sign it may be time to collaborate with others, you learning from their unique contribution and them learning from yours. There will be a joy in teamwork, and The Moirai's presence in your reading is an indication that together you can accomplish something more than you could alone.

This is a time for building, hard work and commitment to a task. It's a good sign that the efforts you have been putting in will eventually pay off.

FALLEN

LACK OF TEAMWORK, DISORGANISATION, GROUP CONFLICT, EGO, COMPETITION

In the inverse position The Moirai card indicates a lack of synergy, each person trying too hard to display superiority or being unwilling to listen to different ways of approaching something. Communications have broken down and you're not functioning as a cohesive unit. Each of the Moirai played a vital function in their team, and each had the same desire and motivation in their role. There is something to be learned here: perhaps you need to be the first to reach out and open up channels for everyone to be heard and considered.

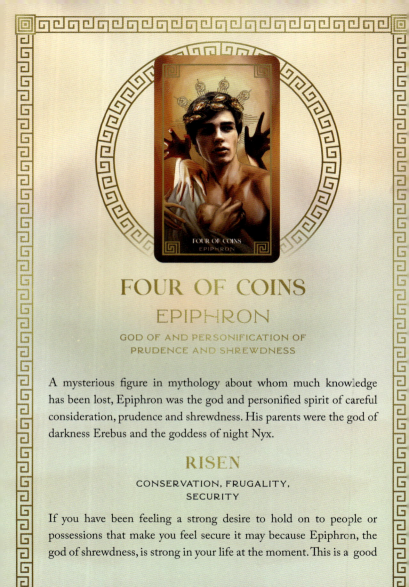

FOUR OF COINS

EPIPHRON

GOD OF AND PERSONIFICATION OF
PRUDENCE AND SHREWDNESS

A mysterious figure in mythology about whom much knowledge has been lost, Epiphron was the god and personified spirit of careful consideration, prudence and shrewdness. His parents were the god of darkness Erebus and the goddess of night Nyx.

RISEN

CONSERVATION, FRUGALITY,
SECURITY

If you have been feeling a strong desire to hold on to people or possessions that make you feel secure it may because Epiphron, the god of shrewdness, is strong in your life at the moment. This is a good time to examine your relationship with money and materialistic possessions: on one hand you may be building a nest egg, ready for long-term security in a very positive manner, yet this card may also be a warning about a scarcity mindset, of you being guided by fear of loss. Remember to respect and honour wealth to ensure a secure future but to not lose sight of what is most important to you and your higher values.

FALLEN

GREED, STINGINESS, POSSESSIVENESS, COVETING MONEY, DECLUTTERING

The fallen position of Epiphron may bring a release from his influence over shrewdness and prudence, leaving you to re-evaluate what is important to you. Perhaps in the past you placed too much value on items and possessions, or you may still find yourself coveting money and possessions in an unhealthy manner. Reconnect with other things you value, such as love and other relationships. It can be a good time to declutter, finding peace in the evaluation of whether items serve you or not.

On the flipside your ties to prudence may be reversed in this reading, and instead of holding on to savings for long-term security money may be slipping through your fingers, causing stress. In the spirit of re-evaluation, look at your spending habits and make sure you are considering the world you're building for your future self.

FIVE OF COINS

PENIA

GODDESS OF AND PERSONIFICATION OF POVERTY AND NEED

Penia was the personified spirit and goddess of poverty and need, her opposite being Plutus, the god of wealth.

RISEN

NEED, POVERTY, INSECURITY, TEMPORARY HARDSHIP, ADVERSITY

Often an unwelcome presence in life, the goddess of poverty and need Penia has appeared in your reading, which suggests a time of hardship, loneliness or loss. An upside is that this is not a card of permanence and that this, too, shall soon pass. It may also indicate a lack of reciprocated feelings from someone you care deeply about or a poverty of attention that you may be craving. Be wary of your health and take time to care for yourself, as your health may not be at its peak.

In the hardships of this card is a reminder to reach out to those around you or even a professional, and not be too proud to accept help. The darkness will pass, but you do not have to pass through the darkness alone.

FALLEN

RECOVERY, CHARITY, IMPROVEMENT, FORGIVENESS, OVERCOMING ADVERSITY

In the fallen position the removal of Penia from your life is a positive one. A change is coming, indicating recovery from previous hardships or illnesses that befell you. You may feel as though your luck has finally turned, and positive thoughts are starting to make their way back into your life. You could find your relationships have taken a turn for the better and that connecting with other people has become easier on a wave of newfound forgiveness.

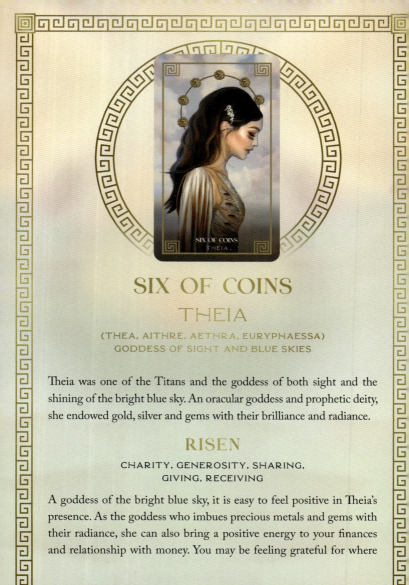

SIX OF COINS

THEIA

(THEA, AITHRE, AETHRA, EURYPHAESSA)
GODDESS OF SIGHT AND BLUE SKIES

Theia was one of the Titans and the goddess of both sight and the shining of the bright blue sky. An oracular goddess and prophetic deity, she endowed gold, silver and gems with their brilliance and radiance.

RISEN

CHARITY, GENEROSITY, SHARING,
GIVING, RECEIVING

A goddess of the bright blue sky, it is easy to feel positive in Theia's presence. As the goddess who imbues precious metals and gems with their radiance, she can also bring a positive energy to your finances and relationship with money. You may be feeling grateful for where you are in life and in a place in which you are able to share your fortunes with others. You're still close enough to the memory of hard times to be able to empathise with those still in them, leaving you with a more generous mindset. This may not just be via the sharing of monetary or physical goods; it can also be a precursor to monetary wealth, time and wisdom.

On the flipside, you may be the one who is receiving benefits from the generosity of others who are helping you get back on your feet so you can eventually pay the kindness forward.

FALLEN

STRINGS ATTACHED, STINGINESS, INEQUALITY, FAKE CHARITY, RECOVERY

The sky is clouded over at the moment, and Theia's light in your life has dimmed. The positive energy of her blue skies and endowment of metals and gems is in reverse, and instead you may find yourself in less than ideal luck with your finances. A giving of money, time or effort might have been unexpectedly one way. Be conscious of your own debts and wealth before giving to others, as you must be able to look after yourself before looking after others. Taking this clouded sky as a break in responsibilities that blue skies sometimes bring means you can engage self-care, especially if you have been giving parts of yourself away for a while.

SEVEN OF COINS

CALLIOPE

(KALLIOPE) GODDESS AND MUSE OF MUSIC, SONG AND DANCE

Foremost of the nine Mousai (Muses), Calliope was the muse of music, song and dance and the patron of epic poetry.

RISEN

HARD WORK, PERSEVERANCE, CREATIVITY, INSPIRATION, FEAR OF FAILURE, GREATNESS

As with great poets, writers and artisans, effort and investment are needed to create great works. Calliope was a goddess who spurred people on to great heights by endowing them with the spirit to create. She can assist you by bringing you inspiration to keep up the effort needed to generate great things. Take a step back from the smaller details and see what you can devise from the bigger picture. It is crucial to make sure you have the patience to finish what you started.

You may have a fear of failure; however, Calliope is here to ease those fears and remind you that you can always learn from any mistakes, that greatness takes time and to fear is human. To perceive in the face of fear is to transcend human limitation and strive towards the divine.

FALLEN

WORK WITHOUT RESULTS, DISTRACTIONS, LACK OF REWARDS, CREATIVE BLOCKS, LACK OF WILLPOWER

Without Calliope's inspiration you may find your ideas and efforts are scattered, or perhaps you have been sinking your time into something that is not bearing fruit and you may need to turn your focus elsewhere. A creative block could be in place that may be hard to shake. This can manifest as a lack of will to create, or as you pouring your essence into something to no avail. It may be time to re-evaluate your approach and goals or find ways to reconnect with your energy and inspiration to galvanise your purpose and application.

EIGHT OF COINS

CHIRON

IMMORTAL CENTAUR

Chiron was a centaur, though it should be noted that unlike his kin he was neither violent nor savage. He was famous for his wisdom and knowledge of medicine, instructing many Greek heroes such as Heracles, Achilles and Asclepius. Chiron renounced his immortality after suffering great and unending pain from a stray poisoned arrow shot by Heracles, yet he lives on in the stars as the constellation Centaurus.

RISEN

APPRENTICESHIP, PASSION, HIGH STANDARDS, MASTERY, PRODUCTIVITY, EDUCATION

As the ultimate teacher and mentor, Chiron's presence in your reading indicates that you may be about to embark on a journey of apprenticeship or mastery. You could have already been working hard to improve your skills or thinking to engage in new studies, embracing concentration and a determination to master what you will be learning. This is also a reminder that you must be prepared for the journey ahead, as your skills do not appear overnight.

If you have no thoughts at the moment for further studies this may be a gentle reminder to explore fresh skills that may better you and give you leverage to achieve your future goals.

FALLEN

LACK OF PASSION AND INSPIRATION, PERFECTIONISM, LACK OF PROGRESS, FURTHER SKILLS NEEDED

In the fallen position this card may indicate you are taking on the role of the wayward student, with Chiron trying to lead you back to the right path. Perhaps you have focused too heavily on perfection. Remember it is okay to surrender to the iterative process of imperfection rather than seeking the myth of perfection. You may also find that a project you have been working hard on has been withholding the results you desire, or you are experiencing feelings of frustration or stagnation. This card in your reading may be the indication that you need to upskill or seek out further learning to help you progress.

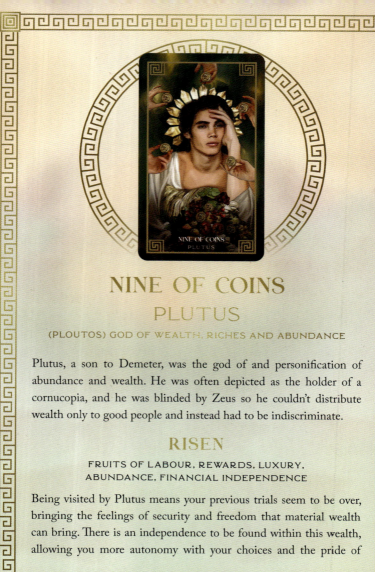

NINE OF COINS

PLUTUS

(PLOUTOS) GOD OF WEALTH, RICHES AND ABUNDANCE

Plutus, a son to Demeter, was the god of and personification of abundance and wealth. He was often depicted as the holder of a cornucopia, and he was blinded by Zeus so he couldn't distribute wealth only to good people and instead had to be indiscriminate.

RISEN

FRUITS OF LABOUR, REWARDS, LUXURY, ABUNDANCE, FINANCIAL INDEPENDENCE

Being visited by Plutus means your previous trials seem to be over, bringing the feelings of security and freedom that material wealth can bring. There is an independence to be found within this wealth, allowing you more autonomy with your choices and the pride of knowing you made it here by your own hard work. You also know the journey you went through to get here and intend to enjoy each day that passes in this new state of comfort.

As with the cornucopia that Plutus holds you may feel a harmony with the beauty and abundance found in nature. Now is a good time to reconnect with the roots of the earth.

FALLEN

RECKLESS SPENDING, LIVING BEYOND YOUR MEANS, FALSE SUCCESS, OVERWORK, SUPERFICIALITY

Having this card in the fallen position means Plutus's abundance is missing from your life, and it may be indicative of financial issues. It could be a warning to watch out for false displays of security and stability, whether that may be from self-deceit or purposeful deceit from others. While abundance and wealth can be easily related back to finances, remember that it goes so much deeper than coins and that wealth can be found in all aspects of life such as a richness of love and happiness.

This card may also be a warning that you are striving too hard for the riches of the cornucopia, overworking to achieve wealth that you have no time or energy to enjoy when there is already a bounty in front of you.

TEN OF COINS

TYCHE

(TYKHE) GODDESS OF FORTUNE, CHANCE AND PROSPERITY

Tyche, the goddess who presided over chance and fortune, was protective of individuals and families and was often moderated by Nemesis, the goddess of retribution.

RISEN

LEGACY, CULMINATION, INHERITANCE, ROOTS, FOUNDATIONS, STABILITY

Tyche, the goddess presiding over prosperity, has brought fortune to you in this completion of your journey. You may achieve abundance through dedication and hard work, and will be blessed in turn. There is a sense of commitment that may come from this success and a desire to make sure it brings permanence rather than short-term gains.

With this success you may feel an urge to articulate your experience, being generous with your loved ones and finding ways to share the positive results with them. Within love, this can be reflected in a strong foundation that you may feel within each other.

FALLEN

FLEETING SUCCESS, LACK OF STABILITY AND RESOURCES, LOSS, CHANCE, GAMBLES

Nemesis is hovering over Tyche's shoulder, moderating her blessings of fortune over you. She is trying to warn you that your future finances may be about to change, and now is the time to evaluate to make sure they stay healthy, balanced and true to your original values. This may signal that you are placing too much stock in your short-term success and pleasures, ultimately harming your long-term potential.

In relationships, Nemesis may signal a dissatisfaction about who you are spending time with, leading you to want to take a chance at better fortunes elsewhere and believing the grass is greener on the other side. This is not always the case, so sit back and reflect on your true feelings on the matter.

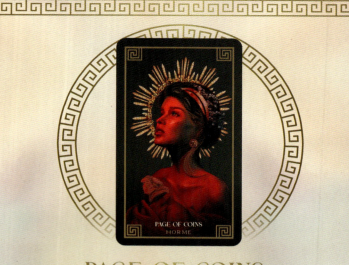

PAGE OF COINS

HORME

GODDESS OF AND PERSONIFICATION OF EFFORT

A mysterious figure in mythology about whom much knowledge has been lost, Horme was the goddess of energetic activity, impulse and effort.

RISEN

AMBITION, DESIRE, DILIGENCE, EFFORT, SOLID BEGINNINGS, GROUNDWORK

As the goddess of effort Horme has appeared in your reading to help lend you her energy to complete what is needed in your current work. When channelled correctly it can enhance your focus and ability to stick to a particular task, helping you achieve your long-term goals. Now is a good time to lay the foundations for future success, as often the groundwork can take the most effort before seeing reward. Within love, whether in a relationship or seeking it, this may be a reminder to put in a little bit more effort before expecting to reap the rewards.

FALLEN

LACK OF COMMITMENT, LAZINESS, NO FOLLOW THROUGH, PROCRASTINATION

With Horme turned from you, you may struggle to find the effort and focus you need to ensure you finish tasks. This could appear via a feeling of being overwhelmed due to exhausting demands or finding yourself distracted by an inability to muster the effort to generate follow through. If you are unable to find Horme's spirit then perhaps ask for assistance or delegate rather than trying to do it all yourself.

If a new project or idea is unable to get off the ground it may be time to step away and re-energise to find the effort needed to get it moving.

KNIGHT OF COINS

ZEPHYROS

(ZEPHYRUS) GOD OF THE WEST WIND

Zephyros was one of the four seasonal wind gods, the Anemoi, bringing in the west wind and the first signs of spring. He competed for the love of a young man with Apollo, ultimately succumbing to jealousy and generating a tragic end to the rivalry.

RISEN

EFFICIENCY, HARD WORK, RESPONSIBILITY, LOYALTY, SMALL GOALS, MUNDANE TASKS

As the bringer of the west wind and spring, hard work and diligence to duty comes with the spirit of Zephyros. This everyday duty may manifest in your life as routine and a kind of general hard work you experience in your day-to-day life. Even when the winds seem mild and their constant blowing repetitive, over time you will reach your goals. Success can happen in a quiet but equally lovely way.

FALLEN

BOREDOM, APATHY, IMPATIENCE, DISENCHANTMENT, FEELING STUCK

Zephyros in the fallen position indicates a reversal of his diligence and godly dedication to bringing the wind. You may desire rewards and recognition without having the willingness to put in the mundane work that is needed. Be inspired by the quiet commitment of Zephyros in his duties, ensuring that you can see the eventual beauty of spring at the end of your journey.

There is also a mischief to the winds. You may be able to bring joy back to your tasks by letting a little bit of spontaneity surround you without you veering off course.

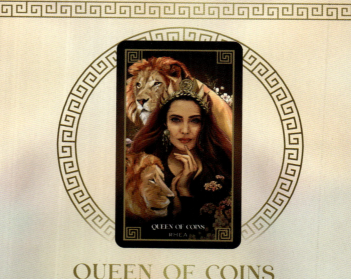

QUEEN OF COINS

RHEA

GODDESS OF FEMALE FERTILITY AND MOTHERHOOD

Rhea was wife to Cronus and mother to many of the Olympian generation. She rebelled against her husband when, to forestall a prophecy that he would be overthrown by his child, he swallowed his children. Rhea assisted one of her children, Zeus, to save his siblings and thus fulfil the prophecy.

RISEN

PRACTICALITY, NURTURING, MULTITASKING, SENSIBILITY, GENEROSITY, GROUNDEDNESS

A card of motherly natured Rhea as the goddess of motherhood brings to earth the skills to play many roles needed to keep family and loved ones happy. Her passion for her children may bring a desire in you to take care of those around you or it may manifest as someone in your life with all these attributes taking care of you.

With motherhood comes a strength that is often underappreciated. Rhea was a strong, powerful woman, and you may find that you have the skills to confidently multitask, execute plans or successfully embark on new ventures.

FALLEN

SELF-CENTREDNESS, JEALOUSY, SMOTHERING, SELF-ABSORPTION, NEGLECT

With Rhea in the fallen position, instead of turning your nurturing energy to others you are instead finding ways to take care and provide for yourself. You still have her strength and mothering nature but it is currently turned inward. Building a strong, independent future in which you are self-sufficient can be highly advantageous, then you can take care of others. There is a warning, however, that you may be taking this inward development too far, neglecting duty of care and becoming absorbed. Find a way to reconnect with Rhea, to discover the balance between taking care of yourself and being able to nurture those around you.

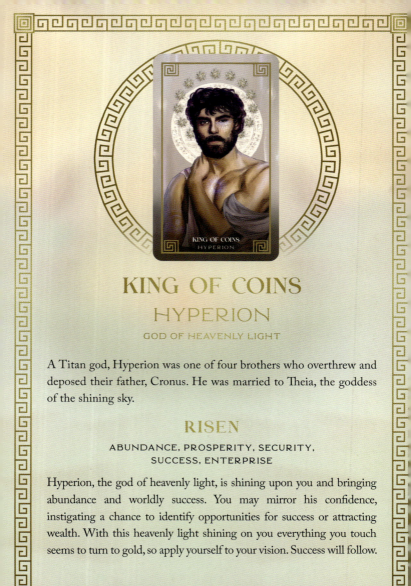

KING OF COINS

HYPERION

GOD OF HEAVENLY LIGHT

A Titan god, Hyperion was one of four brothers who overthrew and deposed their father, Cronus. He was married to Theia, the goddess of the shining sky.

RISEN

ABUNDANCE, PROSPERITY, SECURITY, SUCCESS, ENTERPRISE

Hyperion, the god of heavenly light, is shining upon you and bringing abundance and worldly success. You may mirror his confidence, instigating a chance to identify opportunities for success or attracting wealth. With this heavenly light shining on you everything you touch seems to turn to gold, so apply yourself to your vision. Success will follow.

Hyperion's light may also be lighting up a period in your life when you have fulfilled a task, whether that be creative, business or investment focused. You can now enjoy the rewards of what you have accomplished and the success you have worked for.

FALLEN

GREED, INDULGENCE, POOR JUDGEMENT, INSTABILITY, MATERIALISM

The light that Hyperion brings in the fallen position highlights some spiritual corners that have been cut, leading to delays or the failure of your goals. Perhaps you have been focusing too much on the material aspect of things and not their true value. You may have been mismanaging wealth and not exercising enough self-discipline to ensure that more does not go out than comes in.

On the other hand, Hyperion may be bringing a warning that you are putting wealth above all else and forgetting the light that is found beyond it. Take a moment to consider your relationship with money: is it serving you and your higher values or does it require some thought and change?

CUPS

ACE OF CUPS

PONTOS

(PONTUS) GOD OF AND PERSONIFICATION OF THE SEA

As the primordial god of the sea Pontos represented the sea itself, rather than just being a god residing within it. He fathered many of the sea deities including his granddaughter Amphitrite, Poseidon's wife.

RISEN

NEW FEELINGS, SPIRITUALITY, INTUITION, LOVE, FRESH BEGINNINGS, CREATIVITY

Feel the waves of cool water touch your soul and allow Pontos to wash away emotional baggage from the past to make the most of the bright future ahead of you. With this card, as with the other aces in the tarot, there is an indication of new beginnings and a fresh start.

The swift seas always bring new currents to wash away the old, allowing in a wave of compassion for others, positive emotions and different relationships; it is up to you to open your heart and receive them. For creatives the waters of inspiration may be flowing freely, so now is a great time to start a project.

FALLEN

EMOTIONAL LOSS, BLOCKED CREATIVITY, EMPTINESS, SELF-LOVE, REPRESSION

In the fallen position the oceans are still washing past you, but this time you are the one pulling the tides. It is time to look inward, as the waters are trying to tell you that instead of sending waves of love out you need to send them within. You may be repressing your emotions, so let them flow freely. Do not be afraid of the flood: you have Pontos's powers of controlling the waters and can find ways to release them slowly and privately if you need to. Now is a time for self-love and finding time to fill up your cup before it freely flows back out.

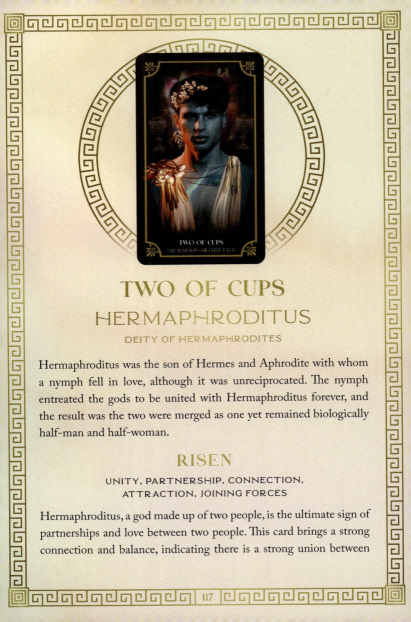

TWO OF CUPS

HERMAPHRODITUS

DEITY OF HERMAPHRODITES

Hermaphroditus was the son of Hermes and Aphrodite with whom a nymph fell in love, although it was unreciprocated. The nymph entreated the gods to be united with Hermaphroditus forever, and the result was the two were merged as one yet remained biologically half-man and half-woman.

RISEN

UNITY, PARTNERSHIP, CONNECTION, ATTRACTION, JOINING FORCES

Hermaphroditus, a god made up of two people, is the ultimate sign of partnerships and love between two people. This card brings a strong connection and balance, indicating there is a strong union between you and another. This may manifest romantically or as a business partnership or a strong friendship. Enjoy this harmony in your life as Hermaphroditus shines brightly. Two are often stronger than one, so take the opportunity to see what heights you can build together.

FALLEN

IMBALANCE, BROKEN COMMUNICATION, TENSION, REJECTION, DIVISION

With Hermaphroditus in the fallen position you may be feeling a lack of harmony either within yourself or with someone with whom you thought you had a strong connection. It is time to find a way to shift your energy flow: be the first to open up conversations in a safe space and you will find that things are easier to repair than they appear to be.

If the imbalance is internal it's time to practise self-love in ways that feel right to you. It is often only when there is self-acceptance, self-love and self-respect that you find the strongest unions with those around you.

THREE OF CUPS
THE GRACES
(KHARITES, CHARITES) GODDESSES OF GRACE, JOY, BEAUTY AND CHARM

The Graces were made up of three goddesses: Aglaia, the goddess of brightness, Euphrosyne, the goddess of joyfulness, and Thalia, the goddess of bloom. They were seen as being the personification of grace and beauty, bringing joy to those they met.

RISEN
FRIENDSHIP, COMMUNITY, HAPPINESS, GATHERINGS, SOCIAL HARMONY

When the three Graces visit you a time of celebration, joy, friendship and creativity has come. They are the goddesses of joy and charm, and they help lift you up and encourage you to connect with your close friends and family to find laughter, love and joy together.

Keep your heart and mind open, soaking in this positive energy and sharing it with those around you.

If you have been having problems with your social life, the Graces may be a sign that these hardships are at an end and that new communication lines may open up to resolve your differences.

FALLEN

OVERINDULGENCE, GOSSIP, ISOLATION, LONELINESS, SOLITUDE

With the lack of presence of the Graces you may find an unbalance within your social circle, with unsaid words lying between you. The usual grace and harmony found within the three goddesses may be missing between you and you may be feeling isolated. You may also find that you've been so busy you've not been able to make time for those you care about, potentially losing touch with friends or growing apart. The Graces are your reminder that friendships need nurturing and effort must be put in to make sure they flourish.

FOUR OF CUPS
STYX

FOUR OF CUPS

STYX

GODDESS OF THE RIVER STYX

Styx was the resident goddess of the River Styx, one of the great rivers that ran through the underworld. Hers were the waters upon which a person must take a ride with the ferryman to the realm of the dead, and her water was the agent of oaths that bound the gods.

RISEN

APATHY, CONTEMPLATION, DISCONNECTEDNESS, MELANCHOLY, BOREDOM

You have found yourself in the River Styx, floating along in a moment of apathy and ignoring the hands that are reaching to help you out. Styx, the resident goddess of this river, is here to give you a gentle push to search your inner truth and find passion again. Things that you currently deem insignificant may lead to wonderful things. Be mindful of new opportunities that arise and make sure you're not dismissing them from a place of negative feelings.

If this card has turned up with Charon, the Eight of Cups, it indicates it is time to journey to your deepest self. This is a powerful combination of gods in a reading that means you can be in control of what you manifest.

FALLEN

SUDDEN AWARENESS, CHOOSING HAPPINESS, ACCEPTANCE, WITHDRAWAL, HEALING

With the River Styx behind you and the goddess Styx in the fallen position it indicates that the slow pull of the river to the underworld is behind you, which could mean either of two things. You may have found your way into the underworld, withdrawn from those around you, so if this is the case then take time away to heal and return when you feel ready, although be wary of shutting out your loved ones. Alternatively, you may have pulled yourself to the shores of the living and feel inspired once more, ready for a fresh start and to embrace new ideas.

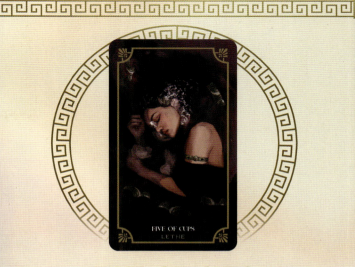

FIVE OF CUPS

LETHE

GODDESS OF THE RIVER LETHE AND OBLIVION

Lethe was the personification and goddess of oblivion and deity of the river of the same name in the infernal regions of the underworld. Those who drank from her shores lost all memory of their past.

RISEN

LOSS, GRIEF, SELF-PITY, DISAPPOINTMENT, MOURNING

You are at the shores of River Lethe and find yourself desirous of forgetting your troubles as you may feel overwhelmed by them. Instead of taking a proactive approach, Lethe is here to ask you whether you are failing to let go of things in your past. You may be so caught up in it that you are incapable of moving on and are missing the new joys that lie in your future.

While Lethe's river cleanses and represents a fresh start free of the past pains of heartbreak and suffering, it is important to also let these hard experiences make you stronger. The easy path out is not always the best, and it may be time to find the inner strength you hold to move on.

FALLEN

ACCEPTANCE, MOVING ON, FINDING PEACE, SELF-FORGIVENESS, POSITIVITY

You have drunk from the River Lethe, and though you have found peace from your troubles she has also granted you key memories for the lessons learned from them. This card can signify a desire to rejoin the world, accepting your past and valuing what you have learned in the larger picture of your life. This is a sign that the past is now behind you so you shouldn't try to undo it. Let go of what doesn't serve you and open your heart to finding positivity about the future ahead.

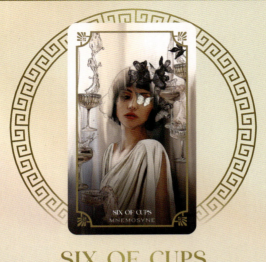

SIX OF CUPS

MNEMOSYNE

GODDESS OF MEMORY

Mnemosyne, one of the Titans, is the goddess of memory and one of the original elder Muses (Mousai). She gave birth to the nine Muses by Zeus and is an oracular goddess with connections to prophecy and oracles.

RISEN

**FAMILIARITY, HAPPY AND CHILDHOOD
MEMORIES, HEALING, FAMILY**

With the goddess of memory Mnemosyne in your reading the veil to the past is thin and memories of it may be strong in your mind. This could be an opportunity to find joy in old pastimes such as hobbies you have put to one side or to reconnect with friends from the past. Let these activities and connections bring you a sense of joy, but do not get trapped within them; we all need to return to the present and avoid living in the past.

If you live away from family you may find these memories bring you homesickness, which may be a reminder to call back home.

FALLEN

MOVING FORWARD, LEAVING HOME, INDEPENDENCE, STUCK IN THE PAST, ROSE-TINTED VIEW

If this card is in the fallen position it may be a warning from Mnemosyne that you are living in a memory. While she may bring visions of the past, it is important to avoid living in them and ignoring the present. You may find you have an inability to move forward from a negative memory or a desire to relive a positive one rather than living in the present. While you should learn from the past, you cannot change it or prioritise it over the now. Celebrate how you have grown and don't mourn the aspects of yourself that have passed. The future ahead of you is bright and you can control how it plays out.

SEVEN OF CUPS

HESPERUS

(HESPEROS) GOD OF AND PERSONIFICATION OF THE EVENING STAR

Hesperus was the personification and god of the evening star and was closely tied with the morning star, Phosphorus (Eosphorus), the bringer of light. Both were embodiments of the star Venus.

RISEN

SEARCHING FOR PURPOSE, CHOICES, DAYDREAMING, INDECISION, ILLUSION

The evening star of Venus and its god Hesperus are bright among the darkness, shining out from the many stars and pathways ahead of you. You are currently searching in the night sky for purpose and dreaming of bigger and better things. Hesperus is here, though, to try to give you his guiding presence in the sky, so you must ensure that you are remaining realistic in your dreams and facing the realities of your current situation and not becoming overwhelmed by the many opportunities in front of you, which may be as numerous and never-ending as the many stars in the sky above you. Make the best possible choices by separating fantasy from reality.

FALLEN

LACK OF PURPOSE, DIVERSION, CONFUSION

With Hesperus missing from the night sky it means you have lost your guiding light and the sky seems dark and distant. You may feel as though you have a lack of options at the current moment or are unclear about what you are searching for. Take a moment to close your eyes and find Hesperus's soft glow within you; he has never left the night sky, even if you can't see it. Use your inner eye to find him and let his light guide your intuition to the correct path once more.

EIGHT OF CUPS
CHARON
（KHARON) FERRYMAN OF THE UNDERWORLD

EIGHT OF CUPS
CHARON
(KHARON) FERRYMAN OF THE UNDERWORLD

Charon was the son of the god of darkness Erebus and the goddess of night Nyx. It was Charon's duty to ferry souls of the deceased over the rivers Styx and Acheron. In payment he asked for a coin, and if the fee was unable to be paid he left the souls to wander the earthly side of the Acheron as ghosts.

RISEN

WALKING AWAY, DISILLUSIONMENT, LEAVING
BEHIND, SELF-DISCOVERY, ESCAPE, TRAVEL

It is time to move from one side of the river to the other as Charon, the ferryman of the underworld, is here to signify the necessity of this transition. You may be drawn to leaving behind worldly worries and actions and embarking on a more spiritual journey, stepping away from the familiar to find a deeper, more rewarding path. If you have been resisting moving on from something, Charon is holding out his hand to help you let go and release that which does not serve you emotionally. This card is powerful when paired with Styx in your reading.

FALLEN

AVOIDANCE, FEAR OF CHANGE, FEAR OF LOSS, INDECISION, DRIFTING

You are currently unwilling to pay the ferryman, uncertain about whether you wish to embark on the journey he offers. The journey ahead may seem complex and you are trying to stay in the world you know, but it has left you stuck in limbo as you hesitate on the shore of the River Styx. Listen to your heart for the next course of action; it may be time to follow this journey with Charon's guidance. Ensure you are boarding the ferry with the right intentions, though, by asking yourself whether there is something you are running away from.

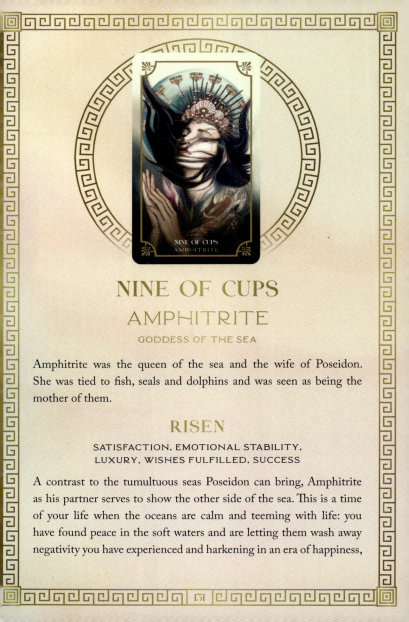

NINE OF CUPS

AMPHITRITE

GODDESS OF THE SEA

Amphitrite was the queen of the sea and the wife of Poseidon. She was tied to fish, seals and dolphins and was seen as being the mother of them.

RISEN

SATISFACTION, EMOTIONAL STABILITY, LUXURY, WISHES FULFILLED, SUCCESS

A contrast to the tumultuous seas Poseidon can bring, Amphitrite as his partner serves to show the other side of the sea. This is a time of your life when the oceans are calm and teeming with life: you have found peace in the soft waters and are letting them wash away negativity you have experienced and harkening in an era of happiness, joy and fulfilment. Focus on gratitude, letting yourself manifest the things you have wished for.

FALLEN

LACK OF INNER JOY, DISSATISFACTION, DISAPPOINTMENT, NEGATIVITY, MISDIRECTION

You have been cast adrift in the sea, assuming that Amphitrite was guiding you, only to realise you are alone and somewhere you're not familiar with. In chasing your dreams and wishes you may have left behind something even more important, so it is time to call for Amphitrite to guide you back through the waters and reconsider what you had originally wished for and realign it with your highest good. Let go of negativity, and remember that even if you cannot see it at the moment the ocean is teeming with life around you.

TEN OF CUPS

NAIADS

(NAIADES) MINOR GODDESSES OF RIVERS, OCEANS AND THE SEA

Naiads were the nymphs of rivers, lakes, streams, springs, fountains and marshes. These minor goddesses are often associated with the goddess Artemis: they protect young girls in their passage from child to adult.

RISEN

INNER HAPPINESS, FULFILMENT, DREAMS COMING TRUE

You have tapped into the large family of Naiads, and their strong community is reflected in your current abundance of love and happiness in your relationships. You feel supported and are experiencing a sense of harmony, and may be inclined to spend more time with family and friends to forge stronger bonds. In combination with Artemis, this can be a powerful card that signifies your time has been spent with a higher purpose in mind.

FALLEN

SHATTERED DREAMS, BROKEN FAMILY, DOMESTIC DISHARMONY

You had thought you were surrounded by peace and that the Naiads had brought you into their fold, but instead you are standing alone at the river's shore. Instead of connections you have found distance, and acts you had taken to bring things together are pulling apart. Find ways to engage with those around you once more, because with communication and honest desires you may be able to reconnect and rebuild. Perhaps you had been chasing the Naiads in the hope of meeting Artemis, so revise your intention behind connections with those whose lives you are a part of.

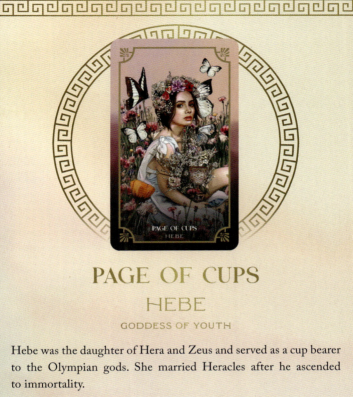

PAGE OF CUPS

HEBE

GODDESS OF YOUTH

Hebe was the daughter of Hera and Zeus and served as a cup bearer to the Olympian gods. She married Heracles after he ascended to immortality.

RISEN

HAPPY SURPRISE, DREAMER, SENSITIVITY, CREATIVITY, INNER CHILD, INNOCENCE

There is a strong call to tap into your inner child and youth, and Hebe as the goddess of youth is here to help you embrace it. With this comes a fresh curiosity and intuitive nature without the prejudices that often spring up as you walk through life. There is magic in the hopeful and wide-eyed dreaming of youth, so this is a calling to channel it back into your life and believe anything is possible. It is time for the creative side of you to be released, especially when in tandem with your emotional side. There is a strong link with creativity with this card, and if you've been thinking of a new creative hobby to start now is the time to do so.

FALLEN

EMOTIONAL IMMATURITY, INSECURITY, DISAPPOINTMENT, MUNDANITY, LOST INNOCENCE

Hebe in the fallen position is here to indicate you have allowed the responsibilities of the past years to weigh on you and you have lost touch with your inner child. The projects you are undertaking may be sheerly for practical purposes, and the initial joy and wonder from them have been forgotten. This is your calling to regain your imaginative spirit, allowing yourself to innocently dream once again. If you find yourself hesitating about plans or a new creative project, try to listen more closely to your intuition so you can understand where the fear is coming from and whether it's justified.

Hebe may also be warning you of someone acting immaturely in your life, acting dramatically or throwing tantrums when things haven't gone their way.

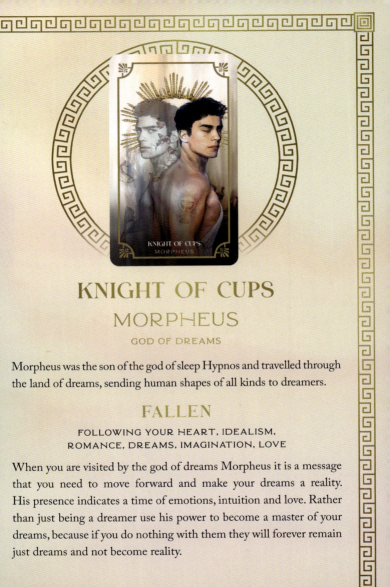

KNIGHT OF CUPS

MORPHEUS

GOD OF DREAMS

Morpheus was the son of the god of sleep Hypnos and travelled through the land of dreams, sending human shapes of all kinds to dreamers.

FALLEN

FOLLOWING YOUR HEART, IDEALISM, ROMANCE, DREAMS, IMAGINATION, LOVE

When you are visited by the god of dreams Morpheus it is a message that you need to move forward and make your dreams a reality. His presence indicates a time of emotions, intuition and love. Rather than just being a dreamer use his power to become a master of your dreams, because if you do nothing with them they will forever remain just dreams and not become reality.

This card is a good omen for romance, which is often the subject of dreamers. It may indicate a new love is on its way to you, or perhaps it is a reminder to keep reality in sight when searching for love. In a relationship there is an indication that something you have been dreaming about may be closer than you think it is.

FALLEN

MOODINESS, DISAPPOINTMENT, DISILLUSIONMENT, BEING UNREALISTIC

The lack of dreams in your life and Morpheus missing from your unconscious mind may leave you feeling moody and frustrated about the lack of time in your life to dream and create. You may find that reality and expectations are getting in the way of you following your heart or enacting plans you had been excited about. This could be a warning that you have found yourself too deep in the dream without the power of Morpheus as a guide and are over-romanticising things and have expectations that are too high. This disillusionment can leave you disconnected from reality. Allow yourself to dream and don't withhold yourself from following them; however, do take a moment to make sure you have considered all the potential outcomes so you can avoid disappointment.

QUEEN OF CUPS

PHOEBE

(PHOIBE) GODDESS OF BRIGHT INTELLECT AND PROPHETIC MINDS

Phoebe is one of the Titan goddesses; her name signifies brightness. She has strong ties to the moon and to prophecy and oracles.

RISEN

COMPASSION, CALMNESS, COMFORT, KINDNESS, WISDOM, SUPPORT

Phoebe, the goddess of bright intellect, is here to help lend her wisdom and help you be the truest, most authentic version of yourself. Her wisdom is manifesting into a deeper understanding of yourself and into finding an inner guide to lead you in the right direction. You may find it easier to communicate with others and be understanding and empathetic to their issues, being heard and understood by them in turn.

While you're in a prime position to help and connect with others there is also a wisdom in self-care and in making sure you focus on your own emotional health so you are more able to help others.

FALLEN

MARTYRDOM, INSECURITY, DEPENDENCE, CO-DEPENDENCY, SELF-CARE, FEELING DRAINED

Phoebe in the fallen position has left your mind wandering, and her sharp guiding wisdom may have left you feeling untethered from a grounding force. You may be experiencing high levels of stress at this time or feel insecure in yourself from chaotic emotions. As the reverse to the risen card, you may still be wrapped up in trying to navigate other people's emotional turmoil and find you have been giving too much of yourself away. This could manifest as a co-dependent relationship, which may be taking an unhealthy turn. See where you can find independence again while still maintaining strong connections that don't drain you.

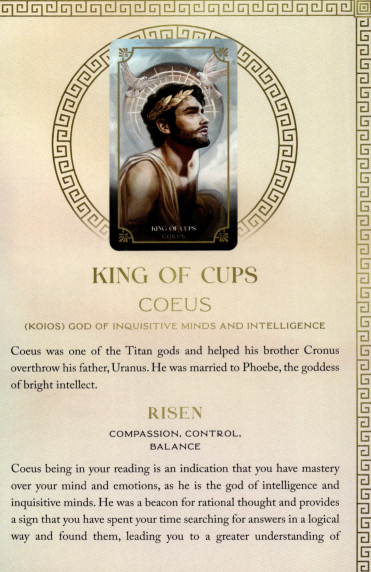

KING OF CUPS

COEUS

(KOIOS) GOD OF INQUISITIVE MINDS AND INTELLIGENCE

Coeus was one of the Titan gods and helped his brother Cronus overthrow his father, Uranus. He was married to Phoebe, the goddess of bright intellect.

RISEN

COMPASSION, CONTROL, BALANCE

Coeus being in your reading is an indication that you have mastery over your mind and emotions, as he is the god of intelligence and inquisitive minds. He was a beacon for rational thought and provides a sign that you have spent your time searching for answers in a logical way and found them, leading you to a greater understanding of yourself. You may be able to use your intellect to navigate and balance the needs of others, bringing harmony to those around you. This may also be a sign from Coeus that you could come across a situation where you must employ these skills and a warning to maintain a level and mature attitude towards your problems. Remain firm in your beliefs without losing your head and don't allow others to steer you off course.

FALLEN

OVEREMOTIONAL, SENSITIVITY, MANIPULATION, HEART OVER HEAD

There is a current imbalance in your emotional state, and Coeus turned from you may be the reason why. You could find that rational thought has gone out the window and you are not in the right space to use your inquisitive mind to search for answers and clarity of self. Your heart may be leading you, leaving you to react to negative energy from others in a purely emotional way. Be careful to avoid immature actions and words at this time.

Be wary also as there may be someone in your life who has become manipulative: while intelligent emotions usually lead to something greater and healthy, in the wrong hands they can be weaponised.

SWORDS

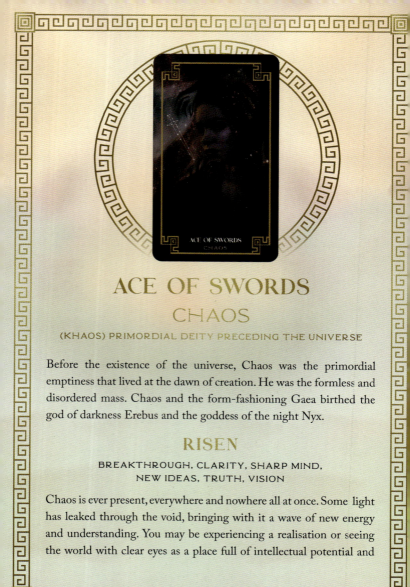

ACE OF SWORDS

CHAOS

(KHAOS) PRIMORDIAL DEITY PRECEDING THE UNIVERSE

Before the existence of the universe, Chaos was the primordial emptiness that lived at the dawn of creation. He was the formless and disordered mass. Chaos and the form-fashioning Gaea birthed the god of darkness Erebus and the goddess of the night Nyx.

RISEN

BREAKTHROUGH, CLARITY, SHARP MIND, NEW IDEAS, TRUTH, VISION

Chaos is ever present, everywhere and nowhere all at once. Some light has leaked through the void, bringing with it a wave of new energy and understanding. You may be experiencing a realisation or seeing the world with clear eyes as a place full of intellectual potential and opportunities to cultivate. Your current clarity in thought puts you in good stead to seek truth and see through deception.

With such a power in your life it is important to act responsibly, taking your next steps in service to others as a partial antidote to the chaotic corruption of power.

FALLEN

CONFUSION, BRUTALITY, CHAOS, MISUNDERSTANDINGS, CREATIVE BLOCK, MISINFORMATION

Chaos is a double-edged sword: holding secrets since before the creation of the universe bred confusion and its eponymous namesake, chaos. Your thoughts may be confused or scattered, leading to poor decisions. Rational thinking rather than impulse is the best way forward, while waiting until the order of insight has been birthed.

You may be the victim of a misunderstanding or make a hasty assumption, so it is worth making the effort to ensure you're not building a foundation out of assumptions.

TWO OF SWORDS
NEMESIS

TWO OF SWORDS

NEMESIS

GODDESS OF RETRIBUTION

Nemesis was a goddess who sought retribution against evil deeds, hubris and undeserved good fortune, keeping the goddess of fortune Tyche in check. In her remorseless dealings with mortals Nemesis helped to maintain the equilibrium.

RISEN

DIFFICULT CHOICES, INDECISION, STALEMATE, MIDDLE GROUND, DIVIDED LOYALTY

Nemesis, a divine seeker of balance, may be in your life to assist you with a hard decision. You could be at an intersection of some kind and lacking the information you need to make decisions both equally good and bad. Let Nemesis remove the blindfold from your eyes so the path forward becomes clearer. She has a deep understanding of balance and justice so she may be able to help you find what tips the scales towards one choice or the other. Until you move past this stalemate there can be no progress.

FALLEN

LESSER OF TWO EVILS, NO RIGHT CHOICE, CONFUSION, STALEMATE, DIFFICULT CHOICES

With Nemesis fallen you may feel as though at this crossroads in your life there is a stalemate and an inability to move forward, as you're stuck between two pathways you don't want to take. Her ability to find divine retribution is absent, and you are uncertain which of the two outcomes will avoid negative repercussions. You may be paralysed by choice, so take a step back and look at the situation from another angle. Explore compromise and consider your first principles and whether your assumptions, goals and advisers are all true.

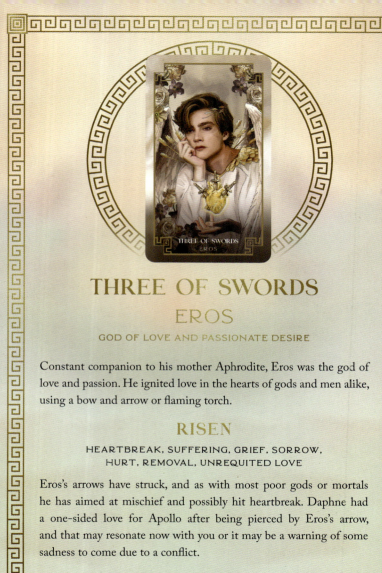

THREE OF SWORDS

EROS

GOD OF LOVE AND PASSIONATE DESIRE

Constant companion to his mother Aphrodite, Eros was the god of love and passion. He ignited love in the hearts of gods and men alike, using a bow and arrow or flaming torch.

RISEN

HEARTBREAK, SUFFERING, GRIEF, SORROW, HURT, REMOVAL, UNREQUITED LOVE

Eros's arrows have struck, and as with most poor gods or mortals he has aimed at mischief and possibly hit heartbreak. Daphne had a one-sided love for Apollo after being pierced by Eros's arrow, and that may resonate now with you or it may be a warning of some sadness to come due to a conflict.

If you are not in love you may still receive a message of rejection, disappointment or hurt in other areas. Remember that pain and grief are necessary parts of life, as they can be turned into lessons. The shadow today is the point of contrast to heighten tomorrow's joy. You might have been knocked down but you can choose to rise again.

FALLEN

RECOVERY, FORGIVENESS, MOVING ON, RELEASING PAIN

In the aftermath of Eros's meddling you may be struggling to move on from a recent loss or heartbreak. This card's presence is a signal that maybe it's time to let go, as there is so much joy to find in life and the sun is still there, obscured as it may be by clouds. Gather your emotions and courage and open the door to new experiences. Allow yourself time to grieve, but also ask yourself what you can do to release the pain and move forward.

On a more positive note, this card may indicate that a silver lining lies ahead. You have passed your time of grief, the future is looking bright and a calm positivity for the future is slowly blossoming after darker clouds.

FOUR OF SWORDS

HYPNOS

GOD OF SLEEP

Dwelling in the realm of Erebus in the underworld, Hypnos was the god of sleep and was often a companion to his brother Thanatos, the god of death.

RISEN

REST, RESTORATION, CONTEMPLATION, SELF-PROTECTION, REJUVENATION, SANCTUARY

The message of Hypnos in your reading is clear: it is time for rest and to rejuvenate. This may be because your battles have been long and hard or because the future is about to throw you your next challenge. Whichever it may be, the need for restoration is apparent. Take time to meditate, withdraw and seek tranquility, doing whatever activity recharges your batteries. Hypnos is here to help ease you into a nourishing sleep, and within that sleep you can develop and marshal your strength.

FALLEN

RESTLESSNESS, BURNOUT, STRESS, RECOVERY, AWAKENING

As with the risen position, Hypnos is here to tell you that it is time to rest. However, in the fallen position it is more akin to a command: you have been overextending yourself and the fight has been taking an unnoticed toll on you. This could be physical or mental, leaving you feeling burned out and empty of emotion. It is time to bow out of the fight, drawing on a self-awareness of your strength to know when to withdraw. Self-love is also important, and with it comes self-care.

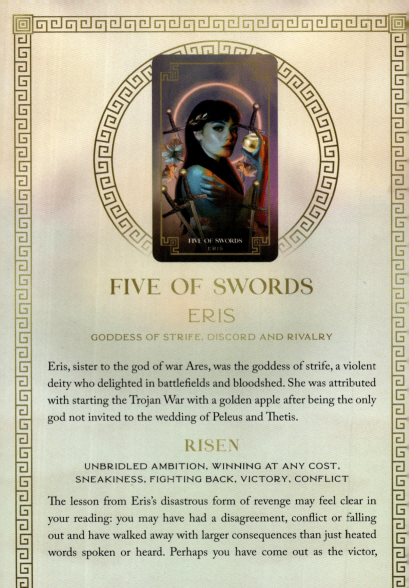

FIVE OF SWORDS

ERIS

GODDESS OF STRIFE, DISCORD AND RIVALRY

Eris, sister to the god of war Ares, was the goddess of strife, a violent deity who delighted in battlefields and bloodshed. She was attributed with starting the Trojan War with a golden apple after being the only god not invited to the wedding of Peleus and Thetis.

RISEN

UNBRIDLED AMBITION, WINNING AT ANY COST, SNEAKINESS, FIGHTING BACK, VICTORY, CONFLICT

The lesson from Eris's disastrous form of revenge may feel clear in your reading: you may have had a disagreement, conflict or falling out and have walked away with larger consequences than just heated words spoken or heard. Perhaps you have come out as the victor, but you need to pay heed to what you have lost. Have any of your relationships become strained? It is time to decide where your values and beliefs lie and to apologise, compromise or reflect lest heated words draw out forge weapons.

If you are true to your highest values Eris may represent standing up for yourself and fighting back, ultimately ending in a validating victory.

FALLEN

LINGERING RESENTMENT, RECONCILIATION, BREAKING A CYCLE, SACRIFICE, COMPROMISE

With her powers of strife and rivalry shadowed, the turned gaze of Eris can be a good omen as it signifies a time to forget and forgive. With the acknowledgement that the road you walk is as important as winning, your energies can be focused on fertile ground for progress and harmony. If there is residual resentment from a recent or past argument it's time to either resolve unaddressed grievances or let them go and move on. Negativity in your life breeds more negativity, so break the cycle and welcome positive energies back into your inner self.

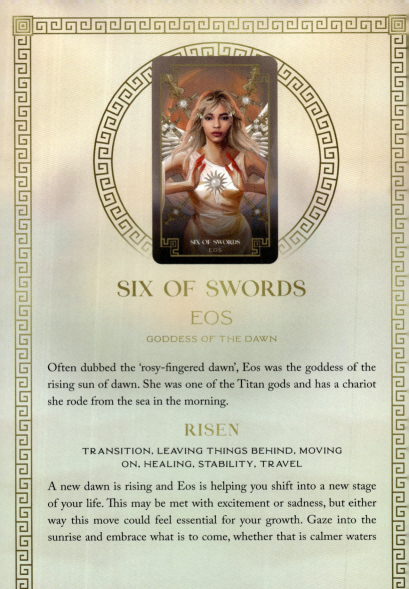

SIX OF SWORDS

EOS

GODDESS OF THE DAWN

Often dubbed the 'rosy-fingered dawn', Eos was the goddess of the rising sun of dawn. She was one of the Titan gods and has a chariot she rode from the sea in the morning.

RISEN

TRANSITION, LEAVING THINGS BEHIND, MOVING ON, HEALING, STABILITY, TRAVEL

A new dawn is rising and Eos is helping you shift into a new stage of your life. This may be met with excitement or sadness, but either way this move could feel essential for your growth. Gaze into the sunrise and embrace what is to come, whether that is calmer waters or fierce rapids. With Eos's rosy-fingered touch lighting up the world, this card can also represent travel or escaping from normal life.

If old hurts have lingered this card may be a sign that you are ready to leave them behind with the dawn light.

FALLEN

EMOTIONAL BAGGAGE, UNRESOLVED ISSUES, RESISTING TRANSITION, CANCELLED TRAVEL, LACK OF PROGRESS

The dawn is rising but you may not be accepting it as the signal of a new day that it is trying to represent. You may be resisting change and transition, especially if you feel they have been forced upon you. Ask yourself why you are not rising with the sun to reach new and exciting heights, and what is holding you back from this crucial transition.

Opposite to the risen form of Eos, her light is touching the far corners of the world but you are not able to enjoy them. Rather than starting a fresh day and journey you may have cancelled travel plans or are currently returning from travel.

SEVEN OF SWORDS

THE ERINYES

(THE FURIES) GODDESSES OF VENGEANCE AND RETRIBUTION

The Erinyes were three goddesses who presided over vengeance and retribution and lived in the underworld, punishing men for crimes against the natural order. They took special care over homicide and crimes against women and of parents upon children.

RISEN

DECEPTION, TRICKERY, TACTICS, STRATEGY, LIES, CUNNING

The Erinyes keep their eternal eye on those who try to ignore consequences, and their gaze has fallen on you or someone in your life. This may imply shadow actions or the keeping of secrets, and although sometimes secrecy is needed in your life you should ask yourself whether the secret is worth the dishonesty, time and anxiety invested to hide the truth and the chance of being found out. If this is not you, listen to your intuition and keep an eye out for changes in behaviour in other people around you. It is important to recognise that secrets can be kept when their owner is not ready to reveal them to the world. Respecting privacy is rarely troublesome.

FALLEN

COMING CLEAN, RETHINKING AN APPROACH, DECEPTION, CONFESSION, PERSONAL AGENDA

As with the three different goddesses who make up the Erinyes there may be three different readings of their fallen position, all of which mean they have their eyes open for potential retribution of the divine. You may have been betrayed, or someone has used your trust to run their own agenda. This card may also be about a renewal of conscience, that you or someone in your circle is about to come clean about something they or you have done.

Finally, it may be a gentle warning that you have been deceiving yourself or trying to fool yourself that everything is okay when it isn't.

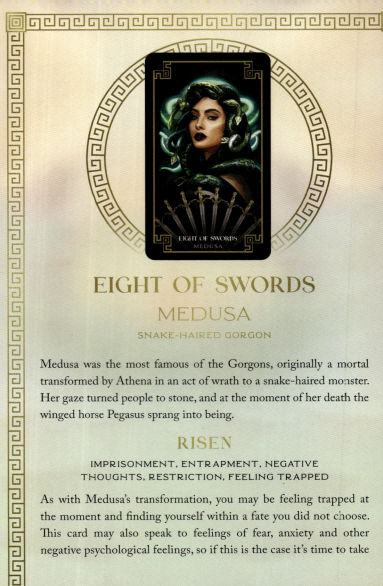

EIGHT OF SWORDS

MEDUSA

SNAKE-HAIRED GORGON

Medusa was the most famous of the Gorgons, originally a mortal transformed by Athena in an act of wrath to a snake-haired monster. Her gaze turned people to stone, and at the moment of her death the winged horse Pegasus sprang into being.

RISEN

IMPRISONMENT, ENTRAPMENT, NEGATIVE THOUGHTS, RESTRICTION, FEELING TRAPPED

As with Medusa's transformation, you may be feeling trapped at the moment and finding yourself within a fate you did not choose. This card may also speak to feelings of fear, anxiety and other negative psychological feelings, so if this is the case it's time to take action rather than giving away your personal responsibility to effect change. Seek help if it's needed, either with the network around you or professional help and especially as your judgement may be clouded. There is a way out of your current predicament; you just need a new perspective.

FALLEN

SELF-ACCEPTANCE, NEW PERSPECTIVE, FREEDOM, SURRENDER, RELEASING FEELINGS

When Medusa is in fallen position it may indicate you are releasing yourself from negative belief patterns. Just as she embraced her powers and being the mighty Gorgon she became, you have opened your life to change and self-acceptance. By refusing to play the role of a victim you can find power within a new state and acknowledge the options in front of you, taking different and exciting paths that weren't open before.

On the flip side, this card may indicate you haven't fully accepted your new self and may be suffering from negative self-talk. While it was a tragic transformation Medusa became incredibly powerful in her new self, and you need to let go of old belief systems and embrace who you are at this time and recognise your own power.

NINE OF SWORDS

PHOBOS

GOD OF AND PERSONIFICATION OF FEAR AND PANIC

Often paired with the god of terror Deimos, Phobos was the god of panic. They accompanied their father Ares into battle, driving his chariot.

RISEN

ANXIETY, HOPELESSNESS, TRAUMA

True to his powers as the god of fear and panic, with Phobos in your reading you may be feeling the effects of his personality. It may relate to past trauma or something that has appeared for the second time. Sharing these feelings with someone could provide you with an outlet for the pain and release you from carrying it alone. As Phobos is a god of internal pains it may be a message to you that your feelings are not reflective of what is happening around you, and instead you are making things out to be worse than they are by overthinking or obsessing about worst-case scenarios.

FALLEN

HOPE, REACHING OUT,
DESPAIR

The light may be at the end of the tunnel with Phobos in the fallen position. You could be at the end of his influence of fear and anxiety and are on the road to recovery, or you may have found help from loved ones or professionals and thus eased your stress and tension.

On the other hand, the fallen position can reflect a very similar message to the risen form of Phobos: you may be experiencing deep inner turmoil brought on by a mindset that is making things out to be much worse than they are.

It is time to seek out people who can help give perspective and hear your feelings, potentially giving you a new way of looking at things.

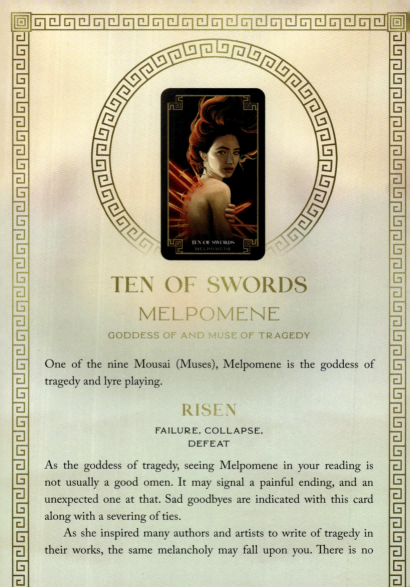

TEN OF SWORDS
MELPOMENE
GODDESS OF AND MUSE OF TRAGEDY

One of the nine Mousai (Muses), Melpomene is the goddess of tragedy and lyre playing.

RISEN
FAILURE, COLLAPSE, DEFEAT

As the goddess of tragedy, seeing Melpomene in your reading is not usually a good omen. It may signal a painful ending, and an unexpected one at that. Sad goodbyes are indicated with this card along with a severing of ties.

As she inspired many authors and artists to write of tragedy in their works, the same melancholy may fall upon you. There is no dishonour in alerting the world to your pain, especially if you couple that song with action. Sharing is often the key to finding the support you need in tough times, and this card may be a warning that you are playing a victim or martyr and hoping for pity rather than a solution to your problems. This card appearing may also be about someone in your life rather than you.

FALLEN

THINGS CAN'T GET WORSE, ONLY UPWARDS, INEVITABLE ENDING

With Melpomene in the fallen position you are either in the middle or the final scenes of your own tragic play rather than the fall before the rise. The more you resist the oncoming fall the more the situation will drag on. Trust that everything that is happening to you can endure, and it is not until you have passed the crucible that you can begin to heal.

If you are instead at the end of your trials, Melpomene's grasp is lessoning and the release from your pain and suffering may soon begin. The particular scene you are in could be coming to an end. Release memories of the past so you can move on to the next chapter with hope for the future.

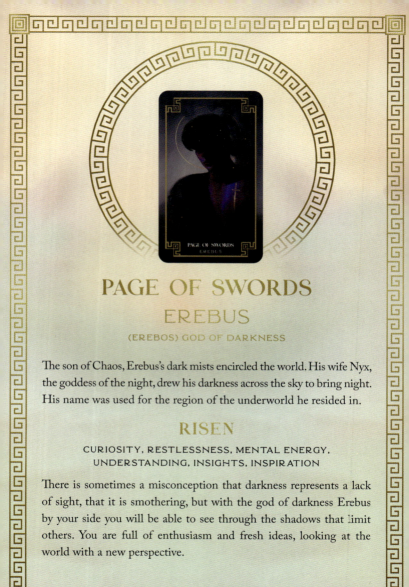

PAGE OF SWORDS

EREBUS

(EREBOS) GOD OF DARKNESS

The son of Chaos, Erebus's dark mists encircled the world. His wife Nyx, the goddess of the night, drew his darkness across the sky to bring night. His name was used for the region of the underworld he resided in.

RISEN

CURIOSITY, RESTLESSNESS, MENTAL ENERGY, UNDERSTANDING, INSIGHTS, INSPIRATION

There is sometimes a misconception that darkness represents a lack of sight, that it is smothering, but with the god of darkness Erebus by your side you will be able to see through the shadows that limit others. You are full of enthusiasm and fresh ideas, looking at the world with a new perspective.

With this revised vision comes a desire to share what you can see with the world, so be open to expressing yourself and discovering different ways to do so. Without a fear of the dark and unknown you will find yourself filled with light, and keen to illuminate for others what you've seen and learned with a strong desire to connect with those around you.

FALLEN

HOLDING BACK, AMBIGUITY, HIDING, DECEPTION, MANIPULATION, ALL TALK

Thanks to Erebus's assistance you are still one with the shadows, able to find clarity and comfort in the darkness, yet when this card is in the fallen position it means you are hiding out of the light, where you find comfort. You may be holding back from expressing your truth publicly or remaining ambiguous on a public issue you have strong feelings about.

This card may indicate you are talking from the shadows but never stepping into the light to follow through. Be careful with promises if you are not going to follow through with them, and avoid deception and manipulation that is used for your own ends.

KNIGHT OF SWORDS

ARES

GOD OF WAR AND THE SPIRIT OF BATTLE

Ares, one of the 12 Olympian gods, was the god of war and the spirit of battle, focusing on the brute force and aggression on the battlefield. This is in opposition to Athena, the goddess of war, who presided over battle strategy and diplomacy. Ares had a steadfast companion in his sister Eris, the goddess of strife, in battle and a great love with Aphrodite.

RISEN

ACTION, IMPULSIVENESS, DEFENDING BELIEF, AMBITION, CHAMPIONSHIP, BRAVERY

The god of war, Ares signals a strong desire for fast thinking and quick acting, moving forward through all obstacles with strength and determination alone. Right now you're being assertive and pursuing a specific goal despite whether or not it's in alignment with your true desires. It is time for bravery, for jumping in and seizing the moment, though you should try to marry this with Athena's battle tactics. With Ares's force alone it can either lead you to find resounding success in overcoming all hurdles or have you charging forth into dangerous grounds.

FALLEN

LACKING DIRECTION, DISREGARD FOR CONSEQUENCES, UNPREDICTABILITY, RELENTLESSNESS, IMPULSIVENESS, BURNOUT

You could be brimming with Ares's energy and lust for action, but there are blocks in your life that mean you can't effectively channel it and you find yourself collared. This may have left you feeling restless or frustrated and resulted in conflict with whoever is holding you back, or you may be experiencing this energy and have an anticipation of soaring excess without proper preparation or planning.

You may not be ready for the speed or force of a furious take off, so it may be time to slow down lest you burn out from exhaustion from the raw energy. Be wary of becoming too ruthless or vicious in your desire to accomplish your goals. The fiercest warrior is the one who has harnessed their fury and has their mind instruct their body to draw their weapon at the right moment. Not obeying your body means that your mind could cut loose.

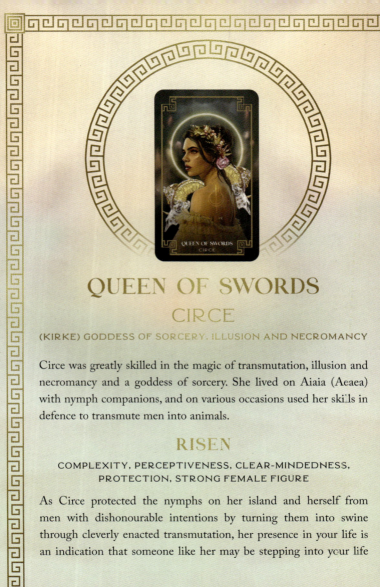

QUEEN OF SWORDS
CIRCE
(KIRKE) GODDESS OF SORCERY, ILLUSION AND NECROMANCY

Circe was greatly skilled in the magic of transmutation, illusion and necromancy and a goddess of sorcery. She lived on Aiaia (Aeaea) with nymph companions, and on various occasions used her skills in defence to transmute men into animals.

RISEN

COMPLEXITY, PERCEPTIVENESS, CLEAR-MINDEDNESS, PROTECTION, STRONG FEMALE FIGURE

As Circe protected the nymphs on her island and herself from men with dishonourable intentions by turning them into swine through cleverly enacted transmutation, her presence in your life is an indication that someone like her may be stepping into your life to help with a problem when you are vulnerable. It could represent someone in your life who is stern and emotionless, but like Circe you will find there is a compassionate side to them once you let them in.

This is a time to lead with your head and not your heart, and you may find yourself connecting with others through intellectual rather than emotional understanding.

FALLEN

COLD-HEARTEDNESS, CRUELNESS, BITTERNESS, PESSIMISM, OVER-EMOTIONAL

In the fallen position Circe may represent an authoritative female figure in your life, although this time instead of protection she is working against you and being demeaning or bitter. Be wary about losing yourself to these emotions and emulating them. Similar to the risen position, Circe provides a reminder to think objectively as your emotions could lead you astray. As with transmutation and sorcery, careful consideration of the tasks ahead is essential right now.

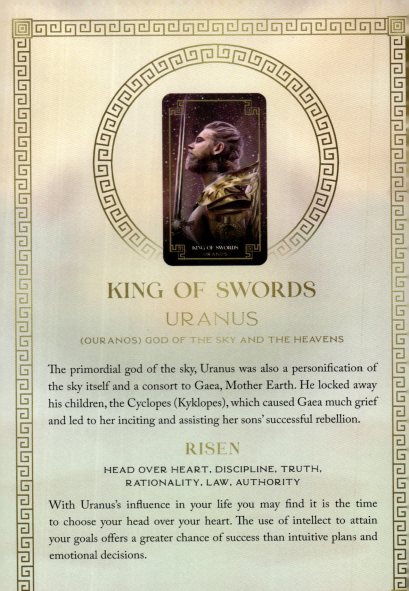

KING OF SWORDS

URANUS

(OURANOS) GOD OF THE SKY AND THE HEAVENS

The primordial god of the sky, Uranus was also a personification of the sky itself and a consort to Gaea, Mother Earth. He locked away his children, the Cyclopes (Kyklopes), which caused Gaea much grief and led to her inciting and assisting her sons' successful rebellion.

RISEN

HEAD OVER HEART, DISCIPLINE, TRUTH, RATIONALITY, LAW, AUTHORITY

With Uranus's influence in your life you may find it is the time to choose your head over your heart. The use of intellect to attain your goals offers a greater chance of success than intuitive plans and emotional decisions.

Where Uranus's wife Gaea is connected to emotions and feminine energy, Uranus is logical and masculine. You may be holding high ethical standards, so look around you and make a decision with impartial logic. With this insight you could be able to accurately categorise your challenges into those you are equipped to address and those that need further preparations. You may need to seek the help of an expert.

FALLEN

MANIPULATIVENESS, CRUELNESS, HARSH INTELLECT, IMPATIENCE, ABUSE OF POWER

While intellect can help you at this time there is a balance to be found. Uranus's cold, harsh rationalisation of the banishment of the Cyclopes ended up turning his family against him, because he alienated them with his unfeeling logic. You may need to watch to see if you are being too impatient with or uncaring to those around you. Work on your feelings and demonstrations of restraint, empathy and forgiveness.

Uranus may serve as a sign to be conscious of the misuse of power in your life or in the lives of others close to you. Ensure you are not the cause.

ACKNOWLEDGEMENTS

This deck is dedicated to my beautiful spiritual community, which made so much art in my life possible, and to Gabby, who was the beginning of it all.

I couldn't have done this without my wonderful husband Paul, who is a never-ending fountain of inspiration, written words and guidance. Thank you to my family and closest friends for believing in me while simultaneously telling me off for creating impossible deadlines for myself.

To the amazing team at Rockpool Publishing: you have been an incredible joy and pleasure to work with. Thank you for taking a chance on me.

ABOUT THE AUTHOR AND ILLUSTRATOR

Helena Elias transformed her career as a senior fashion designer into her personal dream: forming meaningful art. Working with an array of traditional and modern companies, she has helped to support charities that promote women's rights and has had her work featured in TV commercials, live exhibitions and billboards in Times Square. She lives for her work and the reflections of life her work gives to others.

Helena works constantly on moving and evolving with the modern artistic scene, which has resulted in her having her digital non-fungible token work acquired by notaries such as Pranksy & Associates and Keith Grossman, the president of *Time* magazine. She exerts herself to ensure a genuine artistic experience and has long been present in the online spiritual and witch community, where her artistic collaborations have allowed countless women to express their identity not as they are told it should be but from the deep core of their own self-image.

@helena.illustrated | helenaillustrated | helenaillustrated.com